# God's Will, Man's Will and Free Will

# God's Will,
# Man's Will
# and
# Free Will

**Horatius Bonar**
**Jonathan Edwards**
**Jay P. Green, Sr.**
**Charles H. Spurgeon**

*Authors For Christ, Inc.*
*P.O. Box 4998*
*Lafayette, IN 47903*
*Http://www.SovGracePub.com*

*Printed In the United States of America
By Lightning Source, Inc.*

# GOD'S WILL, MAN'S WILL, AND 'FREE-WILL'

## 1. INTRODUCTION

These letters are little more than fragments. They do not aim at a complete statement of the truth, or a systematic arrangement of it. It is only a few important points that they touch. To have extended them and embraced a wider range of doctrine would not have suited my design. I wished to warn you against some of the prevailing errors of the time, lest you, being *"led away from your steadfastness"* should follow after the *"diverse and strange doctrines"* of these last days. So it was necessary to dwell upon those errors which have been most prominently advanced, and to open up those truths which have been most perverted and denied.

My appeal is to the Word of God. What are the reasonings, or opinions, or inferences of men? What is the chaff to the wheat? saith the Lord. Let the Bible decide each question. It is for this that I have appended to each letter a selection of passages at length.

The real question of the present day is just this, Is man a totally and thoroughly depraved being by nature? Is he ruined, helpless and blind, dead in trespasses and sins? Many other questions have arisen, but this is the central one. According to the views we entertain regarding this will be our views upon other points. It is upon the truth of this doctrine that the whole Bible proceeds. And so modify or abate or dilute the statements of Scripture on this point.

Man being thoroughly depraved in nature, is it possible, I ask, to save him without a special and direct intervention of the Father, Son and Spirit, in his behalf? In other words, can he be saved in any way which does not involve personal election by the Father, particular redemption by the Son, and direct, immediate, overcoming operation of the Holy Spirit? Or, putting the question in another form, using the language of science — given a totally depraved being, is it possible to save that being by any plan which makes the previous concurrence of his own will an indispensable preliminary, or which makes it necessary that he should take the first step in the matter of return to God? If you place the different errors of the day before you in this light, you will find that they all more or less deny or encroach on the doctrine of man's original, actual depravity.

You will find, also, that the objections urged against God's sovereignty and man's helplessness, are just different manifestations of human pride, — the pride into which Satan tempted Adam, *"you shall be as gods,"* and into which all his offspring have fallen along with him. Man will not consent to be nothing, that God alone may be all. And it is curious to observe that the objections urged against these truths are not passages of Scripture, but human reasonings — man's inferences and opinions. Take, as a specimen, the doctrine of God's sovereignty. We have passages broadly declaring this, but not one setting forth the opposite. How, then, do men contrive to deny this truth? They begin to reason and speculate upon it; and by means of certain inferences of their own, they try to make it appear inconsistent with other doctrines to which they attach great importance. They say, "Does not God invite the sinner to come to Christ, does He not tell us that He has no pleasure in the death of the wicked, but rather that he should turn and live? Now how can this be true if He is absolutely sovereign in His proceedings? We cannot reconcile these things together, therefore we must explain away the passages which assert God's sovereignty and electing will. They cannot be understood in their plain and literal sense; we must devise some other meaning for them which will accord with our ideas of God's love." So, pride of intellect, confidence in human reason, eagerness to establish one favorite doctrine and to make everything bend to it, supersede and overturn the Word of God. Scripture is not implicitly relied upon, unless borne out by the systems or the syllogisms of reason and the conclusions of man's poor fallen intellect.

3

Cleave, then, to the Word of God. Distrust your own heart, *"lean not to your own understanding,"* but *"receive with meekness the ingrafted word."* *"The world through wisdom did not know God,"* and we must stoop to *"become fools, so that we may become wise."* The *"natural man does not receive the things of the Spirit of God, for they are foolishness to him, for they are spiritually discerned."*

## 2. GENERAL PRINCIPLES

*"Do not be carried about with different and strange doctrines, for it is good for the heart to be established with grace,"* (Heb. 13:9)

You seem bewildered amid the opinions of the day, almost as much as you would be in the midst of a company where each spoke in a different tongue. The difficulty of judging what is truth seems to be increasing, instead of disappearing. You know not what to think, nor which way to turn; in order to discover who is right, or where certainty is to be found; so many novelties stagger and amaze you. There seem to be good men on both sides, and that perplexes you still more. You long for peace amid the jar of these unruly elements, and for stability amid these shifting sands. Yet rest does not come. There is no end of change. One novelty begets another, and that in turn becomes equally productive. One error requires another to maintain it, this second must have a third or fourth to lean on. One false step leads to twenty, or perhaps to a hundred more. Who knows where all this is to end?

The changes are numerous. Every month produces some new doctrine, or at least some modification of the old. Fickle minds lie in wait for something new. As the edge of one novelty wears down, another must be provided in its place to keep up the unhealthy excitement. This fickleness becomes doubly fickle by being gratified; novelties multiply and the sore evil spreads. Men do not tremble at the thought of falling into error. To change opinions upon some casual impulse, or some shallow catch of argument, is thought but a light thing; as if falling into error were no great matter, instead of being a fearful calamity; or as if the entrance upon a truth were an indifferent occurrence, instead of being the occasion of deep and solemn joy. Many who but lately were high Calvinists are now Arminians of the lowest grace, passing through the different levels with the most singular facility and flippancy, as easily and airily as the musician runs up and down the scale with the finger, or the voice.

How is all this, you will ask. It might be enough to answer that it is written, *"in the last days perilous times shall come. For men shall be lovers of their own selves, covetous, boasters, proud . . . led away with different kinds of lusts, ever learning and never able to come to the knowledge of the truth"* (2 Tim. 3:1-10). *"For the time will come when they will not endure sound doctrine – but having itching ears, they will heap up teachers to themselves according to their own lusts. And they will turn away their ears from the truth and will be turned to fables"* (2 Tim. 4:3,4).

But let us inquire a little further. There seem to be chiefly three reasons for this: first, the souls are not at rest; secondly, the consciences are not at work; thirdly, there is little *"trembling at the Word."* I might refer to others, but these are the most prominent ones.

1. THE SOUL IS NOT AT REST. There is a resting-place for the weary – deep and broad, immovable and sure – Jesus, the sin-bearing Lamb of God. But these unstable ones have not reached it. They speak much of it, talk as if they knew everything about it, as if none could state the gospel as freely as they. Yet it is manifest that they have not realized that stable peace which comes from the knowledge of the living Jesus. They are not at rest. And the mind cannot be at rest until the soul is at rest. It will always be making vain fetches after new opinions, in the hope that this or that new doctrine may perchance bring the peace which it has hitherto sought in vain. Be assured of this, that a mind not at rest bespeaks a soul not at rest. And whatever men may affirm to you about their assurance or their peace, if you see them ever on the watch, ever on the wing for some new opinion, you may be sure there is little rest within. In many cases it may be vanity,

attachment to a sect, desire for proselyting others, or simply self-will. But in most cases I have no doubt that it is really in quest of peace that these poor souls are stretching out their weary hands, ready to embrace anything that will fill the dreary void, and pour over their souls that settled calm and sunshine to which (in spite of all their profession) they are really strangers. They are not fastened to the anchor cast within the veil, or else they have let go their hold. And so they are drifting from place to place in quest of anchorage, but they are unable to find it. They try, by means of change, to allay the fever and fretfulness of an unsettled spirit, yet all the while they boast of their assurance, and perhaps censure you sorely if you cannot speak their language and assume their tone.

2. THE CONSCIENCE IS NOT AT WORK. The conscience has far more to do in receiving or rejecting opinions than many suppose. It should stand like a sentinel at the door of the mind, to try all truth before it enters. A tender conscience is cautious and often times very slow in admitting truth, and, on this very account, most tenacious in holding it fast. So, a child of God, with a tender conscience, is often slower in receiving truth than others. For it has to do with conscience in his case. It has to pass into the mind under a watchful eye, which fears to be rash and hasty and trembles at the thought of giving entrance to error. A conscience asleep, or seared, or secure, makes quick work. A specious objection is presented to some old truth, or a plausible argument in favor of some new opinion, and, forthwith, the former is thrust out, the latter taken in, without any resistance or delay, or trembling on the part of the conscience, or any light and guidance from God, sought and obtained upon the matter.

Nothing is more needed in our inquiries after truth than a watchful jealousy of a tender conscience. Yet how little there is of conscience at all in these last days! There is what is called independence of mind, or thinking for one's self, but there is no conscience. It is not waiting upon God for teaching. It is trusting in our own heart, and taking the guidance of our own eyes. It is not "ceasing from man," but the mere pretence of it. It is ceasing from one man in order to trust in another, from one age to trust in another, and that other perhaps the most deceitful of all — our own. So there is such running after novelty, such readiness to receive any plausible error, such self-willedness and headstrong precipitance of judgment, such highmindedness, pride, censoriousness of others. There is so little thought of our own foolishness and fallibility, so slender a sense of the awful responsibility we are under to God, for what we believe for ourselves and propagate among others, as His precious and eternal truth.

3. THERE IS LITTLE TREMBLING AT THE WORD. It is a solemn thing for a man to be spoken to by God, the God of heaven and earth. Each word coming from His lips should be listened to and received with profoundest reverence. *"The Lord has spoken"* is enough for us. There is no room for question or cavil where His voice is heard. Each word in the Bible is to be dealt with as a sacred thing, as a vessel of the sanctuary, not to be lightly handled or profanely mutilated, but to be received just as it stands. There may be passages difficult to reconcile, doctrines which apparently conflict with each other. But let us beware of smoothing down, of hammering in pieces, one class of passages in order to bring about a reconciliation. Let us be content to take them as they are. We shall gain nothing by explaining them away. God has spoken them. God has placed them there. They cannot really be at variance with each other. The day is coming when we shall fully understand their harmony. Let us wait till then, and meanwhile tremble at the thought of misinterpreting or distorting so much as one jot or tittle. Most assuredly we shall not bring about the agreement in any such way. We are only widening the breach and opening but new difficulties.

If I am asked, how can you preach a free gospel and yet believe in election, I answer, I believe in both and preach both because I find both in the Bible; I have no authority for preaching an unconditional gospel but what I find in the Bible. And I have the same authority for preaching an unconditional, personal election. God has told me that both are true, and woe is me if I profanely attempt to mutilate either the one or the other. If one man refuses to take the simple meaning of 'election,' another may refuse to take the simple meaning of "gospel." And were I called upon to say which is the worse, the more profane of the two, I should say the former. I should indeed tremble at the thought of denying either election or the gospel, but I confess that I think the denial of the latter a less direct and less daring insult to the sovereign majesty of Jehovah. It would be a shutting out of His grace, a closing up of all the manifestations of His character which have come to us since Adam sinned. And it would be drawing a dark cloud over our eternal prospects — but it would not be taking the reins of government out of His hands; it would not be the usurpation of His throne; it would not be giving the right hand of fellowship to atheism.

But there is no need of any such comparison. Perhaps it was wrong to make it. I have done so, however, in order that you may be led to see that election belongs to the highest and most sacred order of truths — that it is not a doctrine to be concealed and muffled as if we were either ashamed or afraid of it. It is to be firmly held and faithfully preached, whether men will hear or forbear. Mere philosophy might tell men that, If there is a God, He must be absolutely sovereign in all things. Mere philosophy might expose the shallowness and selfishness of those who trample on God's free will in order to establish man's free will — even if theology and Scripture were silent on the matter.

Why do I preach a free gospel? Is it because reason has revealed it? Is it because I find it suits me best? No! It is because God has declared it. That is my sole authority. Why do I believe in election? Just because God has made it known! I may find that reason confirms this, I may see that there can be no really free gospel without election, but still my ground for believing it is because I find it most plainly revealed.

You can only get rid of election by getting rid of the Bible. And so you will find, among others who deny election and the work of Christ for His church, a great dislike of those passages of Scripture which allude to these topics. They pass them by, they turn away from them, they are angry if another even quotes them, though without a comment. Now I ask, would they do and feel this way if they believed that these passages really contain the meaning which they put upon them? If these passages are quite in harmony with their views, why do they shrink from quoting them, or hearing them quoted? Is this not the plainest of all proofs that they feel that theirs is not the honest interpretation? Does it not show that they themselves are secretly persuaded that these passages do teach unconditional election and the absolute sovereignty of Jehovah? They feel that they have twisted them from their plain sense and that the mere reading of them is enough to expose their distortions. They feel that they have not dealt fairly with the Word of God and that their one-sided dealings cannot bear the light of day.

Let us learn to *"tremble at the Word."* Let us take it plainly and honestly in its simple sense. Let us not be afraid of its apparent contradictions. Let us not think ourselves capable of reconciling and harmonizing all its declarations. We see here but through a glass darkly. The day of light and harmony is coming. All shall then be plain. God will solve our difficulties. Meanwhile, let us reverence every jot and tittle of His holy Word. let us trust our own hearts and reasonings less, God's word more. Let us not be so anxiously asking, How can this be? How can we reconcile God's sovereignty with man's responsibility? How can we harmonize the Spirit's free agency with man's free agency? Let us leave difficulties in the hands of God and let us beware of making those difficulties greater by our miserable attempts to reach at things too high for us, or our miserable efforts to pervert and mutilate the Word of God who cannot lie.

I do not mean, by any of these remarks, to imply that there is not the most perfect harmony between all the different doctrines taught us in the Bible. Nor do I mean to say that this harmony is incapable of being discerned here. I believe on the one hand that all is harmony in the truths of God, and that harmony is discernible and demonstrable even now. But still there is an apparent jar. To a certain extent we can reconcile every one of the supposed discordances. Yet there are difficulties connected with them which no theory can solve, and which will remain difficulties till the great day. To attempt to reconcile or remove these by denying the plain and natural sense of Scripture is sinful and pernicious. It accomplishes nothing. It only takes away one difficulty to replace it with a greater one.

There are doubtless other causes of the evil over which we mourn, but these are the three chief roots of bitterness. To these may be traced more of the manifold errors of our day than many may be willing to allow. Till these are removed, I have little hope that the instability of our times will die out or cease to operate for the injury and subversion of the truth. Till the soul gets rest (not the name but the reality,) and till the conscience is awake and sensitive — and till the word of God is reverenced and honestly interpreted, I see little prospect of an end of these changes — if indeed we may venture to hope that such can be until the Lord comes.

Yet be not amazed, Jehovah changes not, neither does His word. It abides forever, firm as the rocks of the earth, undimmed as the azure of the heavens. Seek to God for light and to His word for wisdom. Take His Holy Spirit as your teacher. Do not heed the jar of man's warring opinions. Let God be true and every man a liar. The Bible is the Bible still. If any man lack wisdom, let him ask of God. You have unction from the Holy One, and you know all things.

Do not be alarmed, as if this were some new thing in the earth. Many speak as if the truth had never arisen among men until they arose to it. But the errors of the day are those of former times. They have shot up once and again and have been as often silenced — and put to shame. They are old and worn out errors; though, perhaps, more daringly set forth now than heretofore. For the time seems at hand in which *"the earth shall reel to and fro like a drunkard,"* and when false teachers and prophets shall deceive, if it were possible, the very elect. Yet do not suppose the attainment of the truth to be a hopeless thing. *"The Son of God has come and has given us an understanding that we may know Him that is true."* It was He who taught the multitudes in the days of His flesh. If He teaches, all is true, all is blessed. Light and knowledge are with Him — and how willing He is that all the light and knowledge should be yours. Learn of Me, He said, for I am meek and lowly. And to what teacher can a foolish, erring soul take himself like this meek and lowly One, who can have compassion on the ignorant, and upon those that are out of the way? He received gifts for men, when He ascended on high, even for the rebellious. And to whom can you go, expect to Him who has the Holy Spirit, with all His gifts and graces, so freely to bestow?

## GOD'S WILL, MAN'S WILL.

*"Shall the clay say to Him that forms it, What are you making? Or your work, He has no hands?"* (Isaiah 45:9).

Having stated what appears to me to be the origin of the theological opinions that are now trying to make way among us, I would briefly advert to some of the principles out of which they spring. I might at once have gone on to discuss the different points or opinions themselves, but I think it may be useful to notice some of the principles which they involve, or what may be called the general aspect and essence of these opinions. We have already seen the soil in which they flourish, we shall forthwith proceed to advert to the branches and fruit. But, before doing so, it may be well to call attention to the roots of the tree. Speaking generally of the new doctrines and the movement which has taken place in connection with them, we may affirm several things.

MAN HAS TOO MUCH TO DO WITH ALL THIS, GOD TOO LITTLE! We hear much of what man does and can do and ought to do. But we by no means hear so much of what God is doing and has purposed to do. Man's agency stands very prominently out of view. God's arm and power are hidden. It seems almost as if man would thrust God aside, take the reins of government out of His hands and be to himself a god. Man gets much credit for doing and saying great things. God gets little glory. The position of the sinner, as a mere receiver of salvation (and every blessing connected with it in this life or the next), is denied. And man is exalted to be a co-operator with God in the matter of salvation. He begins the work by becoming willing, and God ends it. He does what he can, and God does all the rest. He is represented as helping God to save him. Or, rather we should say that God is represented as helping man save himself! In the old creation, God did it all. But in the new creation, as it is a far more stupendous work, He requires the assistance of man. Nay, He commits at least the most difficult and momentous part of it to man himself. If some of the new theories be true, God is not all in all, but is, on the contrary, considerably indebted to man — and man, in like manner, is not a little indebted to himself. In all this we hear still the whisperings of the old serpent, *"you shall be as gods,"* and we see man, like his first father, aspiring to the Divine prerogative.

MAN'S WAY, NOT GOD'S, IS TAKEN AS THE GUIDE OF ACTION. God has a way, a plan, a purpose, well and wisely ordered. This plan which He acts by, He has revealed, and He expects us to take it as our guide in all our schemes. This plan touches and rules things both great and small, nations, communities, churches, with all their movements. Man's wisdom would be to search out this plan, and to shape all his movements accordingly. Inattention to this must not only lead to fruitless efforts and unscriptural schemes, but to much false religion, self-will, formality, excitement and sectarianism. God's design is to glorify Himself, to show the whole universe what an infinitely glorious Being He is. This is His mighty end in all He does and says, to manifest Himself and show forth His glory. For this, sin is allowed to enter the world. For this, the *"Word was made flesh,"* for this the Son of God shed His blood and died. For this, He is taking out of this world a people for Himself. To this all things are tending, and in this shall they be consummated before long. Nothing less than this does God propose to Himself in His doings, and nothing less than this should we ever make our aim and end. All things are but means to this one end. Even the incarnation of His own Son is but means toward an end, but not the end itself. The ingathering of His chosen ones is the means, not the end. The salvation of Israel, the conversion of the world, and the restitution of all things in the day of the coming kingdom shall be the means, but not the end. *"For of Him, and through Him, and to Him are all things; to whom be glory forever."*

Whenever we overlook this, we go wrong and our efforts are but the beating of the air. When we make an end of anything lower than this, we are sure to fall into error. Because when we fix on ends of our own, we are certain to adopt means of our own. Take the case of the conversion of the soul: we cannot be too much in earnest about the saving even of one lost one. I believe we know almost nothing of that deep compassion and yearning love for a dying world, as saints, we ought ever to feel. Yet still it is quite possible to err in this matter, not in being too earnest, but in being so intent on having men converted that we lose sight of the mighty end for which this is to be sought. So the glory of God is hidden from view. And what is the consequence? We cease to look at conversion in the light in which God regards it, as the way in which He is to be glorified. We think if we can but get men converted, it does not so much matter how. Our whole anxiety is, not how shall we secure the glory of Jehovah, but how shall we multiply conversions? The whole current of our thoughts and anxieties takes this direction. We stop to look at both things together, we think it enough to keep the one of them alone in our eye; and the issue is, that we soon find ourselves pursuing ways of our own. Bent upon compassing a particular object, we run recklessly forward, thinking that since the object is right anything that can contribute towards the securing of it cannot be wrong. We thus come to measure the correctness of our plans simply by their seeming to contribute to our favorite aim. We estimate the soundness of our doctrine, not from its tendency to exalt and glorify Jehovah, but entirely by the apparent facility with which it enables us to get sinners to turn from their ways. The question is not asked concerning any doctrine, Is it in itself a God-honoring truth, but will it afford us facilities for converting souls? Will it make conversion a more easy thing, a thing which a man may accomplish for himself and by himself? Will it make conversion less dependent upon God, more dependent upon man? Will it enable us to meet such a text as, *"No man can come unto Me unless the Father draw him,"* and, *"You have not chosen Me, but I have chosen you;" "Can the Ethiopian change his skin,"* etc.

The man who thinks of nothing but how he may (as he calls it) get sinners converted is continually apt to take these devious courses. Impelled but by one force, in one direction, from one motive, he soon errs and loses himself in mazy thickets which, as he plunges on, thicken into deeper intricacy and darkness. Such texts as these present themselves and cross his path. Intent on but one thing, he either shuns them or treads them down. They are incompatible with his one idea, they seem to impede him in the pursuit of his one end. And therefore they must be done away with. It does not occur to him, Am I looking at objects in a partial light, from too low a position, and with a false bias which unfits me for coming to a right judgment? Were such a question asked and answered, as it ought to be, there would be less of one-sided doctrines, misshapen systems, gotten up to accomplish a favorite and engrossing object. Were the glory of the infinite Jehovah seen in its true light, as the mightiest and most majestic of all objects and ends, not to the exclusion of other matters, but simply to their regulation and subordination, then should we be saved the pain of seeing men rushing headlong over Scriptures and reason, striking out strange by-paths of their own, in their eager pursuit of an object on which they have fixed an exclusive and partial eye.

I do wonder at men who have either lost sight of the glory of Jehovah or have made it a subordinate object, or who think that if they can only get men converted then God will look after His own glory. I do not wonder at their being fretted when such texts as those I have referred to confront them in their scheme for facilitating conversion, their desire to make man the converter of himself. A man with only one object in view, and that not the highest, must be stumbled at such declarations and feel at a loss to reconcile them with others. But the man who has set his heart upon the glory of God and views everything in relation to that feels no such difficulty. He has no need to explain away even one verse or clause of the Book of truth. He enters into the purpose of God. He looks at things in the light in which God looks at them. He tries to see them as they might have appeared in the long past eternity — or as they might yet appear in the eternity to come. And he finds all harmony. There is no conflict, no discord at all.

One class of passages show him the yearnings of God's heart over sinful men. They show him that God is in earnest in beseeching men to come to Him. They show him that the sinner's unbelief is the cause of his damnation. They show him that the water of life is free — free to every man, free to every sinner as he stands — and that he is invited to partake, without price or preparation (not only although he is a sinner, but just because he is a sinner). They show him these things and in them he greatly rejoices. He does not wish to abate one jot of the blessed freeness, or cloud the joy of the glad tidings with even one restriction. No, but he takes these passages just as he finds them. He sees how suitable they are to one of the objects on which his heart is set — I mean the conversion of souls. But then he finds another class of passages which follow out another line of truth. They will run him up at once into the purpose and will of Jehovah as the fount and cause of everything great or small. They are quite explicit, just as much so as the other. He can not explain them away. They are so plain and simple that a child may see what they mean. He has no wish to take them in any other than their obvious sense. He sees in them exactly what meets his own feelings and coincides with his view of God's glory as being the paramount and all-regulating end in all the movements of the universe. He does not see in them a restriction on the gospel, but the simple statement of an infinite truth — a truth not arbitrarily thrown across the sinner's path as a stumblingblock, but a truth necessarily arising from the fact that God is God, the Creator, and that man is man, the creature, the sinner. The truth is just this, that God's will is the law of the universe, that His glory is the object and end both in creation and in redemption — His everlasting purpose the mighty and all-perfect mold in which all things are cast, and from which they take their shape and fashion from first to last. In such passages he sees God points out to men the true end which they ought to have in view, and by which all their movements are to be regulated. In them he sees God setting a fence and guard around His own majesty, lest men should imagine that their will is everything, their salvation God's only end, and that in the gospel He has thrown the reins of this fallen earth into the sinner's hands, telling him that everything depends upon his own will and power, that he has to put forth that will and power in order to save himself and restore a ruined world to its former perfection.

Whenever we lose sight of God's great end in all things — His own glory — we fall into a wrong track. We go wrong in judging of doctrine, we go wrong in the formation of our plans, we go wrong in the bent of our efforts. We miscalculate the relative importance of different truths. So our whole tone of feeling, judging and working is lowered and contracted. Zeal for our own ways and opinions takes the place of higher aims. A revival is gotten up to propagate these opinions, or to prop up a sect. Sectarianism and selfish exclusiveness steal in. Egotism, boasting, censoriousness are introduced. Religion becomes an instrument for working out our own views and ends. The most solemn and spiritual things are spoken of with levity and irreverence. Conversion soon becomes the same as the holding of certain opinions. And the mark of an unconverted man is that he rejects these opinions. Being loosened from their anchorage, men drift without a guide. One doctrine after another is embraced. Change succeeds change, as month follows month. To make conversion easy is the great object. And to accomplish this particular end, favorite passages are dealt with incessantly, doctrine after doctrine smoothed over, and Scripture after Scripture perverted or denied.

And after all this toil and change, what is the issue? Is anything gained? Nothing! Scripture has been perverted, man all but deified, and God all but dethroned — but has any difficulty been cleared off, have contradictions been harmonized? No. One class of difficulties has been substituted for another, that is all. The new system gets rid of the alleged contradictions of the old, only to substitute others of its own of a more serious kind. If, for instance, I deny that Christ is truly God, I certainly get rid of the mystery of the incarnation, but the passages which declare His divinity are numerous and explicit. In like manner, by denying the direct operation of the Holy Spirit upon the soul of the sinner, I get rid of the old difficulties concerning man's responsibility, but I substitute for these most serious difficulties as to man's utter depravity, and as to the personal agency and operation of the Spirit. But the old difficulties are to some minds so stale and threadbare as not to be endurable. New difficulties recommend themselves by their freshness and novelty. To get rid of a single old one, some would welcome a hundred new ones.

From such roots many other evils spring, which I cannot enumerate here. There is often manifested a narrowmindedness, a contraction of the spiritual eye, and limitation of the spiritual horizon, which is apt to end in engrossing selfishness. So we often see greater zeal to proselytize to a sect than to win men to Christ. We see great activity displayed in making known and forcing upon others the points on which the difference exists, and much less concern about propagating those in which all believers are agreed. We hear much talking about doctrines and peculiarities, little about Christ Himself. We find conversation turning too much upon the spiritual state of others, and that often in flippance or censoriousness — this one being pronounced unconverted, that one converted — this one being mentioned as having joined the sect, that one as being inclined to join it, or another as standing aloof. We find discussions arising as to whom this one was awakened under, or whom this other, as if this were a matter of any importance, provided the soul is saved and Jesus glorified. We find people extolling the exploits of their ministers, or the doings of their sect, numbering up the conversions that took place at this or that revival under this or that minister, in this or that village or town.

How much selfishness and sectarianism there is in all this! How little there is of simple zeal for the glory of the name of Jesus! A taste for religious gossip, in which the spiritual state of others is freely canvassed, criticized, and decided on, is a very different thing from that relish for the things of God and Christ which shows itself in the saint by the delight which he takes in spiritual converse on things pertaining to God and His glory, to Jesus and His love.

## 3. GOD'S WILL AND MAN'S WILL

*"Cannot I do with you as this potter? says the Lord. Behold, as the clay in the potter's hands, so are you in My hand"* (Jer. 18:6).

Much of the present controversy is concerning the will of God – on this point many questions have arisen. The chief one is that which touches on the connection between the will of God and the will of man. What is the relation between these? What is the order in which they stand to one another? Which is the first? There is no dispute as to the existence of these two separate wills. There is a will in God and there is also a will in man. Both of these are in continual exercise. God wills and man wills. Nothing in the universe takes place without the will of God. This is admitted. But it is asked, Is this will FIRST in everything?

I answer, yes. Nothing that is good can exist which God did not will be to, and nothing that is evil can exist which God did not will to allow. The will of God goes before all other wills; it does not depend on them, but they depend on it. Its movements regulate them. The *"I will"* of Jehovah is the spring and origin of all that is done throughout the universe, great and small, among things animate and inanimate. It was this *"I will"* that brought angels into being and still sustains them. It was this *'I will"* that was the origin of salvation to a lost world. It was this *"I will"* that provided a Redeemer and accomplished redemption. It was this *"I will"* that begins, carries on and ends salvation in each soul that is redeemed. It is this *"I will"* that opens the blind eye and unstops the deaf ear. It was this *"I will"* that awakens the slumberer and raises the dead. I do not mean that, merely generally speaking, God has declared His will concerning these things, but that each individual conversion (nay, each movement that forms part of it), originates in this supreme *"I will"*. When Jesus healed the leper, He said *"I will, be clean."* So when a soul is converted, there is the same distinct and special forthputting on the Divine will, *"I will, be converted!"* Everything that can be called good in man, or in the universe, originates in the *"I will"* of Jehovah. (See James 1:17,18).

I do not deny that in conversion man himself wills. In everything that he does, thinks, feels, he of necessity wills. In believing he wills. In repenting, he wills. In turning from evil ways, he wills – all this is true. The opposite is both untrue and absurd. But while fully admitting this, there is another question behind it, of great interest and moment: Are these movements of man's will toward good the effects of the forthputting of God's will? Is man willing because he has made himself so; or is he willing because God has made him so? Does he become willing entirely by an act of his own will, or by chance, or by moral suasion, or because acted on by created causes or influences from without?

I answer unhesitatingly that he becomes willing because of another and a superior will – God's, that has come into contact with his, altering its nature and its bent. This new bent is the result of a change produced upon it by Him who alone, of all beings, has the right, without limitation, to say in regard to all events and changes. *"I will!"* The man's will has followed the movement of the Divine will. God has made him willing. God's will is first, not second, in the movement. Even a holy and perfect will depends for guidance upon the will of God. Even when renewed it still follows, it does not lead. Much more an unholy will, for its bent must be first changed. And how can this be, if God is not to interpose His power?

But is this not making God the author of sin? No! It does not follow that because God's will originates what is good in man that it must therefore originate that which is evil. The existence of a holy, happy world proved that God had created it with His own hand — the existence of an unholy, unhappy world proves that God allowed it to fall into that state — but it proves no more. We are told that Jesus was delivered by *"the determinate counsel and foreknowledge of God"* (Acts 2:23). God's will was there. God permitted that act of darkness to be done. Nay, it was the result of His determinate counsel. But does that prove that God was the author of the sin of either Judas or Herod? Had it not been for the eternal *"I will"* of Jehovah, Christ wouldn't have been delivered up, but does this give proof that God compelled either Judas to betray or Herod to mock, or Pilate to condemn the Lord of glory? Still further, it is added in another place, *"For truly, against Thy holy child Jesus, whom Thou hast anointed, both Herod and Pontius Pilate, with the Gentiles and the people of Israel, were gathered together in order to do whatever Thy hand and Thy counsel determined before to be done,"* (Acts 4:28). Is it possible to pervert this passage so as to prove that it has no reference to predestination? Does it make God the author of the deed referred to? Must God be the author of sin because it is said that Israel and the Gentiles were gathered together to do what His counsel had determined? Let our opponents attempt an explanation of such a passage, and tell us how it can be made to harmonize with their theory.

It may be argued that God works by means in changing the will. It will be said that there is no need for these special and direct forthputtings of His will and strength. He has ordained the means, He has given His word, He has proclaimed His gospel, and by these means He effects the change. Well, let us see what amount of truth there may be in this. I suppose no one will say that the gospel can produce the alteration in the will so long as the will rejects it. No medicine, however excellent, can operate unless it is taken. The will of man then rejects the gospel, it is set against the truth of God. How then is it made to receive it? Granting that in receiving it there is a change, yet the question is, How was it so far changed already as to be willing to receive it? The worst feature of the malady is the determination not to touch or taste the medicine. How is this to be overcome? Oh! it will be said, this resistance is to be overcome with arguments. Arguments! Is not the gospel itself the great argument? Yet it is rejected. What arguments can you expect to prevail with a man that refuses the gospel? Admit that there are other arguments, yet the man is set against them all. There is not one argument that can be used which he does not hate. His will resists and rejects every persuasive and motive. How then is this resistance to be overcome, this opposition to be made to give way? How is the bent of the will to be so altered as to receive that which it rejected? Plainly by his will coming into contact with a superior will, a Will that can remove the resistance, a will like the one that said, *"Let there be light!"* — and there was light. The will itself must undergo a change before it can choose that which it rejected. And what can change it but the finger of God?

Were man's rejection of the gospel occasioned simply by his misunderstanding it, then I can see how resistance could cease upon its being made plain. But I do not believe that such is the case. For what does it amount to but just that the sinner never rejects the truth. It is only error which he rejects, and were his mistake rectified, he would at once embrace the truth. The unrenewed man then, far from having enmity to the truth (according to this view) has the very opposite! So little of depravity is there in his heart, and so little perversity in his will — such instinctive love of truth and abhorrence of errors is there in him, that as soon as the truth is made plain to him, he embraces it. All his previous hesitation arose from the errors which had been mingled with the truth presented! One would think that this was anything but depravity. It might be ignorance, but it could not be called enmity to the truth. It is rather enmity to error. It would thus appear that the chief feature of the sinner's heart and will is not enmity to truth, but hatred to error and love of truth!

Man's heart is enmity to God — to God as revealed in the gospel, to God as the God of grace. What truth can there be in the assertion that all the sinner's distrust of God and darkness of spirit do not arise from not seeing God as the God of grace? I grant that oftentimes this is the case, I know that it is very frequently misapprehension of God's merciful character, as seen and pledged in the cross of Christ, that is the cause of darkness to the anxious soul, and that a simple sight of the exceeding riches of the grace of God would dispel these clouds. But that is very different from saying that such a sight, apart from the renewing energy of the Spirit upon the soul, would change man's enmity into confidence and love. For we know that the unrenewed will is set against the gospel. It is enmity to God and His truth (Rom. 8:7). The more closely and clearly truth is set before it, and pressed home upon it, its hatred swells and rises. The presentation of truth, however forcible and clear, even though that truth were the grace of God, will only exasperate the unconverted man. It is the gospel he hates, and the more clearly it is set before him, the more he hates it. It is God that he hates, and the more closely God approaches him, the more vividly that God is set before him, the more his enmity awakens. Surely, then, that which stirs up enmity cannot of itself remove it. Of what avail, then, are the most energetic means by themselves? The will itself must be directly operated upon by the Spirit of God: He who has made it must remake it. Its making was the work of Omnipotence; its remaking must be the same, in no other way can its evil bent be rectified. God's will must come into contact with man's will, and then the work is done. Must not God's will then be first in every such movement? Man's will follows.

Is this a hard saying? So some in these days would have us believe. Let us ask wherein consists the hardness. Is it hard that God's will should be the leader and man's will the follower in all things great and small? Is it hard that we should be obliged to trace the origin of every movement of man towards good to the will of God?

If it is hard, it must be that it strips man of every fragment of what is good, or of the slightest tendency to good. And this we believe to be the secret origin of the complaint against the doctrine. It is a thorough leveler and emptier of man. It makes him not only nothing, but worse than nothing, a sinner all over — nothing but a sinner, with a heart full of enmity to God, set against Him as the God of righteousness, and still more against Him as the God of grace, with a will so bent away from the will of God, and so rebellious against it, as not to have one remaining inclination to what is good and holy and spiritual. This man cannot tolerate. Admit that a man is totally worthless and helpless, and where is the hard saying? Is it hard that God's blessed and holy will should go before our miserable and unholy wills, to lead them in the way? Is it hard that those who have nothing should be indebted to God for everything? Is it hard, since every movement of my will is downwards, earthwards, that God's mighty will should come in and lift it omnipotently upwards, heavenwards?

If I admit that God's will regulates the great movements of the universe, I must admit that it equally regulates the small. I must do this, for the great depends on the small. The minutest movement of my will is regulated by the will of God. And in this I rejoice. Woe is me if it is not so. If I shrink from so unlimited control and guidance, it is plain that I dislike the idea of being wholly at the disposal of God. And I am wishing to be in part at my own disposal. I am ambitious of regulating the lesser movements of my will, while I give up the greater to His control. And so it comes out that I wish to be a god to myself. I do not like the thought of God having all the disposal of my destiny. If He gets His will, I am afraid that I shall not get mine. It comes out, moreover, that the God about whose love I was so fond of speaking is a God to whom I cannot trust myself implicitly for eternity. Yes, this is the real truth. Man's dislike of God's sovereignty arises from his suspicion of God's heart. And yet the men in our day who deny this absolute sovereignty are the very men who profess to rejoice in the love of God. They are the ones who speak of that love as if there were nothing else in God but love. The more I understand of the character of God, as revealed in Scripture, the more shall I see that He must be sovereign, and the more shall I rejoice from my inmost heart that He is so.

It was God's sovereign will that fixed the time of my birth. It is the same will that has fixed the day of my death. And was not the day of my conversion fixed as certainly by that same will? Or will any but "the fool" say that God has fixed by His will the day of our birth and death, but leaves us to fix the day of our conversion by our own will. That is, He leaves us to decide whether we shall be converted or not, whether we shall believe or not? If the day of conversion is fixed, then it cannot be left to be determined by our own will. God determined where and when and how we should be born. And so He has determined where and when and how we' shall be born again! If so, His will must go before ours in believing. And just because His will goes before ours, we do become willing to believe. Were it not for this, we should never have believed at all!

If man's will precedes God's will in everything relating to himself, then I do not see how any of God's plans can be carried into effect. Man would be left to manage the world in his own way. God must not fix the time of his conversion, for that would be an interference with man's responsibility. No, He must not at all fix it so that he is converted, for that must be left to a man and his own will. He must not fix how many are to be converted, for that would be making His own invitation a mere mockery, and man's responsibility a pretence! He may turn a stray star into its course again by a direct forthputting of power, and will be unchallenged for interference with the laws of nature, but to stretch out His arm and arrest a human will in its devious course, so as to turn it back again to holiness, is an unwarrantable exercise of His power and an encroachment upon man's liberty. What a world! where man gets all his own way, where God is not allowed to interfere, except in that way that man calls lawful! What a world! where everything turns upon man's will, where the whole current of events in the world or in the church is regulated, shaped, impelled by man's will alone. God's will is but a secondary thing. Its part is to watch events and follow in the track of man's! Man wills — God must say, Amen.

In all this opposition to the absolute will of God, we see the self-will of these last days manifesting itself. Man wanted to be a god at the first, and he continues his struggle to the last. He is resolved that his will shall take the precedence of God's. In the last Antichrist, this self-will shall be summed up and exhibited. He is the king that is to do according to his will. And in the free-will controversy of the day, we see the same spirit displayed. It is Antichrist that is speaking to us and exhorting us to proud independence. Self-will is the essence of antichristian religion. Self-will is the root of bitterness that is springing up in the church — and it is not from above, it is from beneath. It is earthly, sensual and devilish.

## 4. ELECTION

*"Many are called, but few are chosen"* (Matt. 22:14). *"As many as were ordained to eternal life believed"* (Acts 13:48).

You know what a prominent place in Scripture the doctrine of election holds. It meets us everywhere, both in the Old and New Testaments. Whatever may be the meaning of the word, one cannot help feeling that the truth which it expresses must, in God's sight, be a vitally important one. But how can this be the case if it means no more than God's choosing those that choose Him? If it means no more than God's choosing those whom He foresaw would believe of their own accord and by their own power, it is not worthy of the prominent place it holds in Scripture. Nay, it is not worthy of a separate name, least of all such a name as election. If there is any election at all in such a case, it is plainly not God's election of man, but man's election of God. So that the question comes to be simply this: Does election mean God's choosing man, or man's choosing God? It cannot mean both. It must be either the one or the other. Which of the two can any reasonable being suppose it to mean?

As the right understanding of this word is of great importance, I think it well to note down a few passages which will help to shed light on the meaning of the word:

*"The rod of the man whom I shall choose shall blossom"* (Num. 17:5). *"You shall set a*

*king over you, whom the Lord your God shall choose." "The place which the Lord has chosen, to put his name there"* (Deut. 12:21). *"For the Lord your God has chosen them to minister to Him"* (Deut. 21:5). *"Jerusalem the city which I have chosen out of all the tribes of Israel"* (1 Kings 9:32). *"The Lord chose me before all the house of my father, to be king over Israel"* (1 Chron. 28:4). *"For His elect's sake whom He has chosen"* (Mark 13:20). *"He is a chosen vessel unto Me"* (Acts 9:15). *"I know whom I have chosen"* (John 13:18). *"You have not chosen Me, but I have chosen you"* (John 15:16). *"According as He has chosen us in Him before the foundation of the world"* (Eph. 1:4). *"God has from the beginning chosen you to salvation"* (2 Thess. 2:13).

These are but a few out of the many passages that might have been selected. But they are quite enough to show the meaning of the word. No one who wishes to take words plainly, as he finds them, can find any difficulty in understanding what choosing or election means, after reading such passages as these.

I would ask, What does the word election mean in common speech? When we speak of the election of a member of Parliament, do we mean that he first chose himself, then the people chose him because he had chosen himself? Or when we speak of the election of a minister, do we mean that he first chose himself, then the people chose him because he had chosen himself? No such theory of election would be listened to for a moment in such matters. Election has but one meaning there. It means the people's choosing their representative by a distinctive act of their own; or the congregation choosing their representative by a distinct act of their own will. And shall man have his will, but God not have His? Shall man have his choice, but God not have His?

But let us take an instance from the Bible. What does God's choosing Abraham mean? He is a specimen of a sinner saved by grace, a sinner called out of the world by God. Well, how did his election take place? Did not God think of him long before he ever thought of choosing God? Were there not thousands more in Chaldea that God might have chosen and called and saved if he had so pleased? Yet He chose Abraham alone. And what does the Bible call this procedure on the part of God? It calls it election! *"Thou art the Lord, the God who chose Abraham and brought him forth out of Ur of the Chaldees"* (Neh. 9:7). Does anyone say, O, but God chose Abraham because He foresaw that Abraham would choose Him. I answer, the case is precisely the reverse of this. He chose Abraham just because He saw that otherwise Abraham would not choose Him. It was God's foreseeing that Abraham would not choose Him that made election necessary.

And so it is with us. God chooses us, not because He foresees that we would choose Him, or that we would believe, but for the very opposite reason. He chooses us just because He foresees that we would neither choose Him nor believe at all, of ourselves. Election proceeds not on foreseen faith in us, but on foreseen unbelief!

The truth is, election has no meaning if it is not the expression of God's will in reference to particular persons and things. He says to each, You shall be thus and thus, not because you choose to be so, but because I the infinite God see fit that you should be so. To one creature He says, You shall be an angel. To another, You shall be a man. To one order of beings, You shall dwell in Heaven; to another, You shall dwell on earth. To one man, You shall be born in Judea, where My name is named and My temple stands. To another, You shall be born in Egypt, or Babylon, where utter darkness reigns. To one He says, You shall be born in Britain and hear the glad tidings. To another, You shall be born in Africa where no gospel has ever come. So He expresses His will, and who can resist it? Who can find fault, or say to Him, What doest Thou? Men may object at being placed thus entirely at the disposal of God, but the apostle's answer to such is, *"No, but O man, who are you who replies against God?"* (Rom. 9:20). Election, then, is the distinct forthputting of God's sovereign will, for the purpose of bringing a thing to pass; which, but for the explicit forthgoing of that will, would not have come to pass.

But does this not lead to the conclusion that sin is the direct result of God's decree?

Does it not teach us that it is God and not man that produces sin? No. God does not foreordain sin, but He decrees to allow man to sin. God is holy and hates sin. He does not lead men into it; neither does He decree to lead men into it. But He decrees that, for infinitely wise ends, the creature should be permitted to fall, and sin to be perpetuated.

1. God forces no man to sin, either by what He decrees or what He does, either by commanding or constraining or alluring.

2. It is absurd to say that if we hold that God is the author of good, then He must be the author of evil — that if He from eternity purposed to create what is good in man, He must therefore have purposed to create that which is evil. It is absurd to say that if I hold that it is God who sets my will right, then I must hold that it is God who set it wrong.

3. God frequently gave predictions of evil long before the time. Of course, then, if evil is predicted regarding either nations or individuals, then it must be fixed and sure. He predicted the curse on Canaan and his descendants. But does that prove that He was delighted in the curse, or that He was the author of it, or that those who were the instruments of inflicting it, and so fulfilling the prophecy, were guiltless?

4. Even our opponents admit that there are some events decreed beforehand, such as the birth and death of Christ, the Judgment Day, etc. If, then, they admit that He has decreed a single event they are in precisely the same difficulty in which they seek to fix us. If one event is decreed, why not all? Who is to draw the line and say, These are decreed, but these are not? God's will has already fixed one or two, and is man's will, or chance, to settle the rest?

In further explanation of this point, let me quote a few paragraphs from a tract which I published some years ago:

I know that the sinner must have a will in the matter too. It is absurdity to speak of a sinner loving, believing, etc., against his will, or by compulsion. The sinner must will, beyond doubt. He must will to take the broad way, and he must will to take the narrow way. His will is essential to all these movements of his soul. But in what state do we find his will at present? We find it is wholly set against the truth. Every will since the fall is wholly opposed to God and His word. Man needs no foreign influence, no external power to make him reject the truth. That he does by nature. He hates it with his whole heart. When a sinner then comes to receive the truth, how is this accomplished? Does he renew himself? Does he change the enmity of his will by the unaided act of his will? Does he of himself bend back his own will into the opposite direction? Does he, by a word of his own power, cause the current that had been flowing downhill to change its course and flow upward? Does his own will originate the change in itself, and carry the change into effect? Impossible! The current would have flowed forever downward had it not been arrested in its course by something stronger than itself. The sinner's will would have remained forever in depravity and bondage, had not another Will, far mightier than itself, coming into contact with it, and altered both its nature and course, working in the sinner "both to will and to do." Was the sinner willing before this other Will met his? No! Was he willing after? Yes! Then, is it not plain that it was God's will meeting and changing the sinner's will that made the difference? God's will was first.

It was God's will that began the work and made the sinner willing. He never would have willed had not God made him willing. "Thy people shall be willing in the day of Thy power." It is the power of Jehovah applied to us that makes us willing. Till that is applied, we are unwilling. It is His hand, operating directly upon the soul, that changes its nature and its bent. Were it not for that our unwillingness would never be removed. No outward means or motives would be sufficient to effect the change, for all these means and motives are rejected by the sinner. Nor does he become willing even to allow the approach or application of these means or motives till God makes him willing. To speak of his being changed by that which he rejects is as absurd as to speak of a man's being healed by a medicine which he persists in refusing. "Can the Ethiopian change his skin, or the leopard his spots?" (Jeremiah 13:23).

Then are all willing? Doesn't the depraved will remain in most, while the new will appears in few? What makes the difference? God's choice! *"Even so, Father, for so it seemed good in Thy sight." "Has not the potter power over the clay, from the same lump to make one vessel unto honor and another unto dishonor?" "Except the Lord of Hosts had left unto us a very small remnant, we should have been as Sodom and we should have been like Gomorrah".*

Does God then hinder sinners from believing and willing? No, by no means. He hinders none. They are their own hindrance. *"You will not come to Me that you might have life."* Not one soul would be saved if left to his own will. But, in His infinite mercy, God does not leave them to their own wills. He puts forth His mighty power on some to make them willing. Were it not for this, all would be lost, for all would reject the Saviour.

But is this not unjust? Is God dealing fairly with His creatures in making some willing and leaving the rest to their unwillingness? What! Are we to prohibit God from saving any unless He saves all? Are we to accuse Him of injustice because He leaves some to reap the fruits of their unbelief and delivers others from it? Is God unjust in saving whom He will, when all were lost?

*But is this not unjust? Is God dealing fairly with His creatures in making some willing and leaving the rest to their unwillingness? What! Are we to prohibit God from saving any unless He saves all? Are we to accuse Him of injustice because He leaves some to reap the fruits of their unbelief and delivers others from it? Is God unjust in saving whom He will, when all were lost?*

Some are given to accusing us of making God guilty of partiality. As if they were singular in their zeal for God's honor, they exclaim, We cannot bear a partial God. Partiality means of course injustice. It means also that the sinner has a right to favor from God. They must show, then, that for God to save some when all were lost is unjust. They must show that all sinners had a right to His favor, for if none had any right, there can be no partiality. But if this theory is true, then God was partial in not providing a Saviour for fallen angels. He was partial in choosing Israel, and not choosing Egypt or Babylon, as the nation to whom He made Himself known. He was partial in sending prophets to Israel and not to Tyre and Sidon. He was partial in doing His mighty works in the land of Judea. And Jesus was partial in commanding His disciples not to go to either Gentiles or Samaritans. In short, if sovereignty is partial, then the Bible is full of it. And it would be just as well for these men to say at once what their theory implies — that God is not at liberty to act as He pleases, but can do only what man dictates.

But why does God save some and not all? Because such is *"the good pleasure of His will."* He has infinitely wise reasons for this, though we do not understand them. Might we not with equal propriety ask, Why did He keep some angels from falling? And, Why did He allow others to fall? Or, may we not ask, Why did He not think of saving angels, why think of saving men alone? Is Jehovah not at liberty to do what He will with His own? Is He not at liberty to create as many worlds and as many beings as He pleases? And when these are ruined, is He not at liberty to redeem as many or as few as He pleases?

Are all men so depraved that they will not be saved unless God puts forth His mighty power? That is the real question in all this.

If so, then, it is plain that God must put forth His power to save everyone that is saved. And surely He is at liberty to choose whom He is to save. If indeed men are not totally depraved, then there is no need for the interposition of God's hand either in choosing or in saving. But admit man's total depravity and ruin, and you must admit the direct forthputting of the arm of Jehovah. And so it is that many in our day are beginning to deny man's total depravity of nature. They are smoothing down the expressions which do refer to it in Scripture, and claiming for man as much remaining power and goodness as will enable him in part to save himself, to do it without the interposition of God.

The following remarks of Calvin will show that in his day none but "Papist theologians" held the doctrine that God elects men because He foresaw they would believe. "The

Papist theologians have a distinction current among themselves, that God does not elect men according to the works which are in them, but that He chooses those who He foresees will be believers. And therein they contradict what we have already alleged from St. Paul, for he says that we are chosen and elected in Him, *'that we might be holy and without blame.'* Paul must have spoken otherwise if God elected us having foreseen that we should be holy. But he has not used such language. He says, *'He has elected us that we might be holy.'* He infers, therefore, that the latter (faith) depends upon the former (election). Those who think otherwise know not what man and human is." Such is the witness of Calvin against the Papal theologians; since that time many have joined the ranks of these theologians and glory in their heresies.

O, but it is said, we do not deny election. We merely maintain that God elected those whom He foresaw would believe. I answer, this is a total denial of election. And it is dishonesty or ignorance to call this by such a name. God elects those who He foresaw would believe, you say? And who were they? None! Absolutely none! He foresaw that none would believe, not one. And because He foresaw this, He elected some to believe. Otherwise not one would have!

With regard to the foreseeing who would believe, I have some difficulties to state: According to the Arminian theory, I may thus go on believing and disbelieving alternately until the day of my death. God then one day foresees that I will believe, and He decrees to save me. But the next day He foresees me not believing, and He decrees that I should perish. How, in such a case, is the matter to be finally settled? Is it according to the state in which God foresees the sinner will be at the last moment of life? Or when? Let our opponents solve the difficulty, if they are able.

O, but some profane objector says, Does God make men to be damned? Let me in a few words answer the miserable atheism of such an objection . . . It is somewhat remarkable that this is precisely the argument of Socinians, Universalists and Deists against the existence of such a place as hell. If you speak of hell or everlasting fire to such, their answer is, Did God make men to damn them? And however abominable and unscriptural their notion is, it is at least consistent with their own theory. Making God to be all love and nothing else, they think it inconsistent with His love that He should allow such a place as hell in the universe. They do not believe in a hell, so they ask, Did God make men to damn them?

But let me answer the question, however profane it may be. God did not make men to damn them! He did not make the angels *"who kept not their first estate,"* to damn them. He did not make Lucifer for the purpose of casting him out of Paradise. He did not make Judas for the purpose of sending him to his own place. God made man — every man and every thing — to glorify Himself. This every creature, man and angel must do, either actively or passively, either willingly or unwillingly; actively and willingly in Heaven, or passively and unwillingly in hell. This is God's purpose and it shall stand. God may have many other ends in creation, but this is the chief one, the ultimate one — the one which is above all the others, and to which all the rest are subordinate.

In this sense then plainly, God did not make men either to destroy them or to save them. He made them for His own glory. If the question is asked, Did God make the devil and his angels only to damn them, I answer, He made them for His own glory. They are lost forever, but does that prove that He made them to destroy them? He kept their companions from falling, and so they are called the *"elect angels,"* while He did not keep them. But does this prove that He made them to destroy them? They fell, and in a moment they were consigned to everlasting chains. He made no effort to save them, He sent no redemption to them. But does this prove that He made them only to destroy them? If ever such an accusation could be preferred against God, it must be in the case of the angels, to whom no salvation was sent. It cannot be said of man, to whom a salvation has come.

Whatever is right for God to do, it is right for Him to decree. If God's casting sinners into hell is not wrong or unjust, then His purposing to do so from all eternity cannot be wrong or unjust. So that you must either deny that there is a hell, or admit God's right to predestinate who are to dwell there forever. There is no middle way between Calvinism and Universalism.

With these remarks I leave this point, and in doing so I would merely call your attention to one or two passages of Scripture which it would be well for those to ponder who put such a question as that to which I have given an answer:

*"The Lord has made all things for Himself; yea, even the wicked for the day of evil."* (Prov. 16:4).

*"As many as were ordained to eternal life believed"* (Acts 13:48).

*"The Scripture says to Pharaoh, Even for this same purpose I have raised you up, that I might show My power in you and that My name might be declared throughout all the earth . . . what if God, willing to show His wrath and to make His power known, endured with much longsuffering the vessels of wrath fitted to destruction?"* (Romans 9:17,22).

Texts like these are not to be explained away or overlooked. They are part of God's holy word, just as much as *"God is love."* And if one class of texts is to be twisted or turned away from, why not another? Let us look both in the face, and let us believe them both, whatever difficulty we may find in reconciling them.

Our first duty is to believe, not to reconcile. There are many things which in this life we shall not be able to reconcile, but there is nothing in the Bible which we need to shrink from believing.

*"Vain man would be wise, though man be born like a wild ass's colt"* (Job 11:12).

## 5. PREDESTINATION AND FOREKNOWLEDGE

*"Being predestinated according to the purpose of Him who works all things after the counsel of His own will"* (Ephesians 1:11).

It is of some importance that we should settle the real nature of these two things, predestination and foreknowledge to ascertain which of the two is first. The question is, does God fix a thing simply because He foreknows it, or does He foreknow it because He has fixed it? There are vague ideas in man's mind at these points. It is well to know the truth with distinctness. I answer, Predestination must be the foundation of foreknowledge. God foreknows everything that takes place because He has fixed it. In proof:

1. The opposite of this is an impossibility. To fix a thing is to make that thing certain to come to pass, which, but for the fixing would not have happened . . . God knew all that might possibly have come to pass had He let the world alone to act out its iniquity. In all the infinity of possibilities, He saw that the thing He wanted was not to be found. Seeing the end from the beginning, He saw that the thing He desired would never come to pass unless brought into being by a direct act of His own will. No other will would desire or could effect that which He saw to be best, either in regard to persons or events. The thing He wanted was not to be found among the possibilities, but among the impossibilities, if matters were left to themselves, to the operation of the usual laws. How, then shall that which is impossible be rendered not only possible but certain? Evidently by the direct interference of God! God having thus interfered and arranged everything according to His wisdom, of necessity He must know them to come to pass. In other words, He foreknows everything because He has arranged everything. Everything is certain in His foreknowledge because it is so in His arrangements.

Take the case of a saved sinner, such as Saul of Tarsus. In looking forward from eternity, God saw that sinner. He saw him in his guilt and sin. He saw him hastening away from Himself, He saw that if left to himself, or to the usual law of things, Paul would only go deeper into sin and farther from Himself. He saw that in such a case his salvation was impossible – that he never would believe and would never repent and turn. This was all that mere foreknowledge could tell. Foreknowledge alone can do nothing as to salvation. But here predestination comes in. God forms a design to bring man to glory, he is a *"chosen vessel."* And having this design regarding him, he resolves to put forth His power, He pre-arranges all His plans concerning him, He fixes the day and the hour of his conversion, and so He foreknows its certainty — because He has fore-arranged it. Otherwise it could not have been known; nay, it would have been an impossibility.

2. The opposite of this is an absurdity. What can be more absurd than to fix a thing which I already know will come to pass whether I fix it or not? This is truly imputing foolishness to God. It represents Him as giving a solemn decree to fix a thing which is already certain. As if the queen of this realm should decree that the sun should rise tomorrow, because she knows that it will be the case, from the laws of nature. Is it not mockery of God? It makes Him thus to speak, *"I foreordain that a sinner shall be saved, because I foresee that he will be saved."* Unless, then, we impute folly to God, and affirm that there is nothing in the word predestination, we must admit that God must foreordain before He foreknows, and that He knows everything just because He has forearranged everything according to His own infinite wisdom.

These are two arguments which appear to me quite conclusive. But let us turn to Scripture. I do not need to again direct your attention to the passages which were quoted previously. But note two previously quoted, *"Him, being delivered by the determinate counsel and foreknowledge of God, you have taken and by wicked hands have crucified and slain"* (Acts 2:23). *"For truly, against Thy holy child Jesus, whom Thou hast anointed, both Herod and Pontius Pilate, with the Gentiles and the people of Israel, were gathered together in order to do whatever Thy hand and Thy counsel determined before to be done"* (Acts 4:27,28).

1. The language is very explicit and plain. It is the strongest that could possibly have been used to denote foreordination. There is nothing about it ambiguous or hard to be understood. To take it in any other sense would be absurd. The doctrine may be inscrutable, but the words are plain. And is the nature of the doctrine a reason for refusing to take the words of God in their natural sense?

2. Admitting our views of foreordination to be true, could they have been expressed in language different from this, or from that employed in the Epistle to the Romans and Ephesians? Had we been left to choose our words for setting forth our views, we could not have desired any other than these. Can our opponents say the same? Are these words the most appropriate for expressing their views?

3. This determinate counsel is said to have fixed certain events in Christ's history. Now, if some were fixed, we have reason to conclude that all others also were. Yet in the life and death of Christ we see nothing but what seemed outwardly to occur in the natural order of events. It will certainly be conceded that the will of the Son of God was free from first to last. Yet we learn that what He voluntarily did and suffered was also predetermined by God. In His case there was entire free-will, yet entire preordination. What, then, becomes of the objection to predestination, arising from its supposed interference with the free-will of moral agents? In Christ's life and death we have a series of pre-ordained events, and at the same time a series of free actions. And this is sufficient answer to the current objection. We may not be able to reconcile these things, yet they stand palpably before us.

4. This determinate counsel is said to have delivered up Christ into the hands of men. Pilate and Herod, etc., are said to have done what God's hand and counsel had pre-determined. Here is something still more striking. The deeds of these wicked men are said to have come to pass according to this counsel, yet these deeds are no less wicked, and those men are no less responsible. Here, again, we have another objection answered, or at least silenced. To reconcile things may be difficult, yet the statement in this passage is plain. What pride and folly, then, are there in the questions and cavils which we so often hear in connection with this doctrine:

If God has arranged everything, man's will is not free, someone will say. How can the sinner be responsible? How can he be plied with motives and arguments? Of what use is it to do anything toward an end, if all is arranged beforehand by Another? How unjust it is in God to warn and invite sinners when He has fixed everything already! All these cavils have their answer in the passages quoted above. It is vain to think of putting questions such as these until these strong and explicit declarations have been explained away. They teach us plainly that our world's history is a history of events, pre-ordained by God from eternity, yet at the same time coming to pass by the free agency of man. This pre-ordination is the effect and the expression of God's will, yet it does not in the least interfere with man's responsibility. Nor does it suppose any violence done to the will of man.

It was certain that the ten tribes were to revolt, for it was predicted long before. But did it make their revolt less voluntary? It was certain that Christ was to be born at Bethlehem, but did that make the coming of His parents to that town less voluntary? It was certain that Judas was to betray Christ, for it had been predicted by David long before in the Psalms, but did that lessen the sin of Judas or make his act less free? In the same way I might go over every prophecy, and ask the same question. And I wonder greatly what our opponents would answer. How can they reconcile their ideas of free agency with the fact that the sin of Judas was predicted by the Holy Spirit as certain, 1000 years before it came to pass? Was Judas a mere machine? Was God the author of his sin?

But it will be said, Are we not told that this election is according to foreknowledge? (1 Pet. 1:2; Rom. 8:29). In reference to the first passage, I would remark that the word foreknowledge, in the second verse, in the original is the same as that rendered 'fore-ordained' in the twentieth verse. There can be no doubt that it means pre-ordination, for it refers to Christ as the appointed Lamb. And if so, then, it is impossible to suppose that the word foreknowledge in the second verse refers simply to foreseeing and nothing more. But then we are asked to look at Romans 8:29, *"Whom He did foreknow, He also did predestinate to be conformed to the image of his Son."* The word *"foreknow"* means not simply to know before hand, but to fix the choice upon. The meaning is then evidently, *"whom God set His choice upon, them He predestinated to be conformed to the image of His Son."* These saints were the objects of His eternal choice, they were appointed by Him to the honor of being made in the image of His own Son.

I wish to notice some concessions of our adversaries which appear to overthrow their whole system. They admit that in certain things there is a real election. They admit, for instance, that there is a real election of particular nations to particular privileges.

This admission is fatal to their theory. For their main prop was that the election of individuals was just another word for favoritism and injustice. Now, if the election of persons is unjust, that of nations must be more unjust. If the one is inconsistent with man's responsibility, so must the other be. If the election of men shows an undue partiality, much more must the election of nations. For God to reveal Himself to the Jews and not to the Egyptians is as much favoritism as for Him to convert one soul and not to convert another. He did far more for Israel than He did for any other nation. He brought them near Him. He gave them His Word. He taught them the way of forgiveness through the blood of the sacrifices. He placed them in circumstances of peculiar advantage. He did not do this for Babylon or Nineveh, to Assyria or Egypt. Can it be wrong, then, to choose individuals, yet right to choose nations? Can it be wrong not to choose an individual to salvation, yet right not to choose a nation to those privileges through which alone salvation comes? Can it be right to pass by some nations and yet wrong to pass by some individuals? Nations are composed of individuals, and to choose a nation is to give individuals in that nation a peculiar advantage which issues in the eternal life of thousands. And so if there is any injustice in the matter, there is more injustice in a national election than in a personal one. It will be said, God knew what nations would reject His message, and therefore He did not send it to them. On this I offer this:

1. A nation being composed of individuals, our opponents must maintain that God foresaw that every soul in them would reject the truth. If not, would it not be hard, upon their theory for God to withhold the gospel from the whole nation, if He knew that some in that nation would have believed and been saved?

2. If these nations were denied the gospel, because God foreknew they would reject it, then they are condemned for a thing they never did, but which God merely foresaw they would do. Whole nations are treated as criminals, rejecters of the gospel, when the opportunity was never given them either to receive or reject it. I am not aware of anything in Calvinism so hard or unjust as this. We teach that God punished men and nations on account of what they actually do, not on account of what He foresees they would have done if He allowed them the means. This theory, on the other hand, teaches that whole nations are condemned to that most fearful of all curses, a deprivation of the gospel, not on account of their actual sins, but because certain things were foreseen which they would have done! Now, if God can justly condemn nations on account of sin not committed, but merely foreseen as likely to be committed, why may He not condemn sinners to eternal death for sins never committed, but only foreseen? Would this be just? Strange that men should maintain the justice of depriving nations of the gospel for sins which they never committed, yet affirm the injustice of God choosing a soul to everlasting life according to His sovereign will. But this is just one of the paradoxes of Arminianism. God chooses some to life, it is said, because He foresees they will believe. So that it is not faith that saves us, but God's foresight of our faith. Nor is it actually unbelief that ruins us, but God's foresight of it.

3. God speaks of sending His messages to some who would reject, and of not sending it to others who were more likely to have received it, *"For you are not sent to a people of a strange speech and of a hard language, whose words you cannot understand. Surely, if I had sent you to them, they would have listened to you"* (Ezek. 3:5,6). This surely settles the matter — it is not a nation's foreseen willingness to hear that leads God to send His messengers, nor a nation's unwillingness foreseen that prevents Him from sending. It is all according to His sovereign will.

It is affirmed that there is a work equally in the hearts of all men alike. It is said that God has done and is doing the very utmost that can be done for every individual of our race; and that to maintain anything else is to charge God with partiality and injustice, as well as to deny the responsibility of man. The proof adduced in support of these statements is a passage in Isaiah 5, *"What more could have been done to my vineyard that I have not done in it?"* (vs. 4). But it is remarkable that this is one of the strongest proofs that God did a great deal more for Israel than He did for any other nation. He allowed the whole world to remain a wilderness, but He made them His vineyard. He fenced this vineyard. He gathered the stones of it and planted it with the choicest vine. *"He did not deal so with any other nation."* Was this partiality or injustice? Or was this doing the same thing for all?

Besides, it is evident that this passage is being perverted. It doesn't mean that God at that time had done all He could for Israel. For He went on to do much more for them. Not only did He not cease to bless them, but He multiplied His blessings, and increased in strivings with them, long after He had uttered the words here. So that the passage cannot mean that He had done all He could, for He proceeded to do a great deal more, raising up prophet after prophet to give them line upon line. Nay, many of the most gracious words Israel ever heard were spoken after this time. If, then, the verse does really mean that God had actually done His utmost, the inference which is founded upon it falls to pieces.

It is plain, then, that God does more for some nations than for others. He did more for Israel than He did for Egypt or Babylon. He did more for Israel at one time than at another, for one generation than another; for one district of Judea than another; even for one individual than another. What else is the meaning of the words of Jesus, *"I tell you truly, many widows were in Israel in the days of Elijah, . . . but Elijah was not sent to any of them except to Sarepta, a city of Sidon, to a woman, a widow. And many lepers were in Israel in the time of Elisha the prophet, and none of them were cleansed except Naaman the Syrian"* (Luke 4:25-28). Will any of the deniers of God's sovereignty furnish a solution of this passage? In accordance with their views, what can the Lord mean?

It is not true, then, that God does as much for one nation or for one individual as another. The opposite is and always has been the fact — a fact frequently referred to in Scripture as proof of God's right to do according to His will in the armies of heaven and among the inhabitants of the earth (Dan. 4:35). No reasonings of men can alter the fact, nor can any ingenuity deprive the fact of its deep and solemn meaning. I may perhaps be told that the cause of this inequality is in the church of Christ, which has not done its duty. It is said that if Christians had acted aright, the world would have been converted long before now. As this is a common way of attempting to solve the difficulty, it may be well to answer fully.

1. Who told them that the cause is wholly in the church? Who told them that the world would have been converted before now if Christians had been what they professed to be? Give me one single passage of Scripture that states this. Surely it is a bold and hazardous assertion to make, without one verse of Scripture to support it.

2. It is not ture. What! shall such a mighty and majestic event as the salvation of the world be dependent upon a creature's will? Is it to depend upon man whether the world is to be converted or not? Has God no purpose to be carried out? Has He nothing at all to say in the matter? Is He to stand by looking on, wondering if it may please His people to put forth their energies to convert the world?

3. It is unscriptural. There are passages of Scripture which explicitly contradict it. What, for instance does God mean when he gives as the reason why He enjoined Paul to remain and labor in Corinth, *"I have many people in this city"*? Again, what is meant by that similar passage, *"And as many as were ordained to eternal life believed"*? Again, what did our Lord mean when He said, (as if explaining the reason why so many rejected Him) *"Many are called, but few are chosen"*? Or what did He mean when He said, *"The gospel of the Kingdom must be preached among all nations for a witness, and then shall the end come"*? And, lastly, what did the Holy Spirit mean, first by forbidding the apostles to preach the word in Asia, and then prohibiting Paul from going over to preach in Bithynia?

4. It is profane. It is saying that the wickedness of the world cannot be remedied by God, but only by the church; that God has not power to convert the world; that it is the church which has all the power, and that unless she pleases to put forth her might and zeal, God can do nothing for the world. Poor world! This is sad news indeed. Your destiny hangs on the power and love of your fellow-sinners! The strength and love of your God are nothing and can do nothing for you. Miserable comfort and miserable comforters indeed! Yet these are the men who speak so much of the love of God!

Yet I am far from saying that Christians are not much to blame. How little do the most zealous among us do for souls! How much more might we do by prayer, by labor and by holy living. Still, I deny that the inactivity or unbelief of saints will account for the darkness that overspreads the nations. Failure in duty on the part of the people of God may account for many things, but not for all. Did the prophets of old fail in their duty, and was their failure the reason why Nineveh, or Tyre or Sidon were not converted? Was it their fault that they were not sent to these cities and received no message for them? Why were there so many prophets raised up within that small territory and not one commissioned to bear tidings to a dark and dying world? Could none be spared? Could no more be raised up? Did they refuse to go? Had God no message of grace to give them for the dark millions of Europe or Asia or Ethiopia?

Did the Son of God fail in His duty, in that He did not preach the gospel to any but the lost sheep of the house of Israel? Why did He make this distinction? Why did He never travel beyond the narrow Judean circle? Why did He command His disciples at first to make the same difference, prohibiting them from preaching the gospel in the cities of either the Gentiles or the Samaritans? Might not the Samaritans have said, You tell us that the utmost has been done for us that can be done, and that all are equally dealt with. Why then are we passed by? And why are the messengers of peace prohibited from entering our territory? What answer could be given except that such was the will and purpose of the only wise God?

Did the apostles afterwards fail in their duty when, after Pentecost, they went abroad to proclaim the everlasting gospel? Was their failure the reason why the world was not then converted? Are we not plainly taught that such was not the case? Why was it that when Paul wished to go to Bithynia to preach the gospel there, the Spirit would not allow him to go? Was this doing the utmost for Bithynia that God could do? Nay, it was not even the utmost that Paul could have done and wanted to do. If the Spirit works at all, then it is plain that the reason why He succeeded in some and fails in others must either be one of the following reasons:

1. It might be because some have naturally better hearts than others, more inclined towards what is good, made of less rebellious and more believing materials. This better class of sinners, less stouthearted than others, then could be said to yield and obey, and so are saved. The rest being more stubborn and ungodly hold and are lost. What hope does this give to the chief of sinners? Where in all this is there the plucking of brands from the burning?

2. Or, because the Spirit has attempted a work beyond His power He fails in His efforts. The sinner has overpowered Him and proved stronger than He. The sinner is able to overcome the Spirit, but the Spirit is not able to overcome the sinner. The Spirit has done His utmost and has failed.

But, finally, to say that the Spirit is doing all He can possibly do for the sinner is either a mere quibble, a play upon words, or else it is a most melancholy profanity. If it means that literally and truly Omnipotence has been taxed to the utmost and has failed in the attempt to convert a sinner, it is profanity. For it is saying that a creature is mightier than the Creator, able to withstand, nay, able to overcome Omnipotence. If, however, this is not said to be so, then what else can be the meaning but that God is doing all He sees fit to do for each individual? He is putting forth in each the utmost degree of power that His infinite wisdom sees fit. And if this is all that is intended, then there is harmony between us. For what is this but merely another way of stating Jehovah's absolute and all-wise sovereignty in giving or withholding blessing?

"What shall we say then? Is there unrighteousness with God? God forbid. For He says to Moses, I will have mercy on whom I will have mercy, and I will have compassion on whom I will have compassion. So then it is not of him that wills nor of him that runs, but it is of God who shows mercy. For the Scripture says to Pharaoh, Even for this same purpose I have raised you up, that I might show My power in you and that My name might be declared in all the earth. Therefore He has mercy on whom He will have mercy, and whom He will He hardens. You will then say to me, Why does He yet find fault? For who has resisted His will? No, but, O man, who are you who replies against God? Shall the thing formed say to Him who formed it, Why have you made me this way? Has not the potter power over the clay, from the same lump to make one vessel unto honor and another unto dishonor? What if God, willing to show His wrath and to make His power known, endured with much longsuffering the vessels of wrath fitted to destruction? and that He might make known the riches of His glory on the vessels of mercy which He had before prepared unto glory – even us whom He has called, not of the Jews only, but also of the Gentiles?" (Rom. 9:14-24).

# 6. THE WORK OF CHRIST

*"The church of God, which He has purchased with His own blood"* — Acts 20:28.

I do not intend to enter fully upon the subject of Christ's work. This would require a much fuller discussion than I am able at present to bestow upon it. It would in fact require a volume of itself.

Christ is said in Scripture to have given Himself as a ransom and substitute for His church, and to have done so in a way such as He has not done for any other beings. This seems implied in the very first promise — the promise regarding the woman's seed. here we have at the very outset the identifying work of Christ and His people — the setting them before us as entirely one with Him. His destiny and theirs are thus one from the beginning. We recognize here not only the Redeemer, but the chosen people, the people given Him of the Father, with whom He identifies Himself, and in whose behalf He is to die and to suffer — to bruise the serpent's head and to submit to the bruising of His own heel.

It is not merely Christ who is said to have died. His people are said to die with Him. The Apostle Paul very frequently dwells on this idea, representing the church as crucified with Christ, dying with Him, rising with Him, ascending up with Him and sitting with Him in heavenly places. In Jehovah's eye His people were with Him all the time, from His coming into the world. He stood in their stead, and they were viewed as one with Him from His cradle to His cross, and from His cross to His throne. They were taken up to the cross with Him. They died there with Him. They went down to the grave with Him. Now, I confess I cannot understand these expressions unless I believe in a definite number for whom all this was especially done. I cannot see how it is possible for the atonement to be indefinite, so long as I read that in all its parts the church was associated with Christ. This renders definiteness an essential element in the idea of redemption.

But how can there be any truth in all this if Christ has no special object in view in dying, except merely to render salvation possible to all, but certain to none? In that case He could only die as a man for His fellowmen — not as a substitute, not as a representative, not as a surety, not as a shepherd at all. I put it to you, which of these is most in accordance with the Word of God?

It is the view which would present itself to the eye looking from the past eternity into the future, contemplating the glorious issue. And it is the view which we hereafter shall more fully realize when we get into that eternity and begin to look back upon the whole finished scheme. Viewed from either of these points, the far past or the far future, the thing seems striking and vivid. Standing as we do in the present in the very midst of the scenes, with the smoke of the world all around us, seeing but darkly through the glass, we may find it more difficult to realize this. But faith can rise out of these dark elements below. It can transport itself to either of these eternal eminences. And, looking at things as God looks on them, contemplating results as He does, faith will be able to realize God's purpose regarding the church in all the different stages of its progress now, as if it had actually been represented in visible brightness, and the other parts which confuse us hidden from view. The moment the sculptor is hewing out his statue is not the best time to ascertain what he means. You must look at his designs, or you must wait until he has finished his work.

Here are some of the passages which represent Christ as doing a peculiar work on behalf of His church: *"I am the good Shepherd, the good Shepherd gives His life for the sheep"* (John 10:11). *"I am the good Shepherd and know My sheep and am known of mine"* (John 10:14). *"I lay down My life for the sheep"* (John 10:15); *"You do not believe because you are not of My sheep"* (John 10:26); *"Thou hast given Him power over all flesh so that He should give eternal life to as many as Thou hast given Him"* (John 17:2). *"I pray for them, I do not pray for the world, but for those whom Thou hast given Me"* (John 17:9). *"Husbands, love your wives, even as Christ also loved the church and gave*

*Himself for it"* (Ephesians 5:25).

In these passages we hear Christ repeatedly speaking of those whom He calls sheep, and telling us He gave His life for them — for them in a peculiar sense, as He did for no other. It is as a shepherd that He died with a shepherd's love and a shepherd's care — for His sheep as such. Again, He prays for His own, for those whom the Father has given Him, not for the world. Can words be plainer? Here is certainly a distinction made, *"I pray not for the world."* Here at least is something peculiar to His church alone. And one such peculiarity is enough to answer the objections of adversaries. Is not the way in which He prayed an illustration of the way in which He died? Are not those for whom He prayed the same as those for whom He died?

But over against all this are set those many passages in which the word *"all"* occurs, as in *"Christ died for all."* Now the passages already quoted are more explicit and cannot be overthrown. They are too plain to be mistaken. Yet there are admittedly some difficulties with regard to some of the passages in which the word *"all"* occurs. But it is better to confess the difficulty and wait for further light than at once to proceed to do violence to the passage itself, or to make its difficulty a reason for doing violence to others.

With regard to the meaning of the word *"all"* in the Bible, especially in the N. T., a few remarks will be necessary. It occurs there more than 1200 times. These 1200 texts may be subdivided:

Class I consists of a very large number of passages, several hundreds, in which it is undeniable that the word cannot mean *"all"* literally. To give one or two specimens, we are told that *"all"* the land of Judea . . . went out to him and were all baptized." This was certainly not literally the case, for every individual in the whole land did not come, for we are expressly told that *"the Pharisees and lawyers were not baptized by him"* (Luke 8:30). Again we read, *"all men seek Thee"* (Mark 1:37). This was not literally so. Every individual in the human race, or even every individual in Judea, did not seek Him. Again, we have such passages as these, *"He told me all that I ever did"* (John 4:20); *"all things are lawful to me"; "all our fathers were under the cloud"; "all those who are in Asia have turned away from me";* and, *"you know all things."*

Class II consists of passages in which it is very doubtful whether all is literally universal. It may, or it may not be. There is nothing positively to determine it. *"Every nation under heaven"; "All those who dwelt in Asia"; "The care of all the churches"; "All who dwell on earth shall worship him"* (Acts 2:5; 19:10; 2 Cor. 2:28, etc.) These are specimens of a large class of doubtful passages, which, of course, can prove nothing as to the literal meaning of *"all".*

Class III consists of passages which are only determined by the context, not by the expressions themselves. The whole passage taken together fixes the meaning. But were it not for that, the literal meaning would have been doubtful. *"you are all brothers"; "All these things shall come to pass", "they all slumbered"; "When Jesus had finished all these sayings,"* etc. In all these passages and in many similar ones, it is not the word *"all"* itself that points out the strict universality, but it is some other word that occurs along with it, such as *"all these things".* In these cases, while in one sense the word has a universal sense, in another it has a limited one — limited by the words with which it is connected. It means all of a certain class, all of a certain number. So that we gather from these that when *"all"* is to be understood literally, we must learn from the context what the word means — whether it is all of one nation or all of another, whether it is all of one class or all of another. This answers at once the oft-repeated argument which consists merely in vociferating the word *"all"* as if the loudness or the frequency of the outcry were enough to demonstrate the meaning of the word. That meaning must be determined in each separate case by the other words, or parts of the passage.

Class IV consists of the passages in question, those supposed to imply a universal atonement. On these I cannot enter here. They are the fewest of all the four classes. Our opponents say they must be interpreted literally. Let us see how the proof stands.

Of the Scriptures in which the word *"all"* occurs, a large number are exceedingly doubtful. Another large number are only proved to mean literally *"all"* by the context. The fewest in number of these four classes are those which are claimed by our opponents.

The result of this statement is simply this, that the mere occurrence of the word *"all"* does not determine the question at all. Nothing but a careful examination of the whole passage can settle it. Do not then be deceived by the loud repetitions of the words – all and every – when intended to take the place of more solid proof.

It is impossible to do more here than to notice one passage, being one of the strongest and one that affords an admirable illustration of the need for looking at the context to determine the meaning of the word. It is, *"He tasted death for every man"* (Heb. 2:9). It is literally *"for each,"* since there is nothing about men in the original Greek. The question then arises, what does the apostle mean by *"each"*? The context must settle it. It either carries us back to the *"heirs of salvation,"* or forward to the *"many sons."* For obviously it must refer to some of whom the apostle was speaking. Now, he was only speaking of the angels, and of the many sons, the heirs of salvation, and of no other. It cannot be the angels, therefore it must be the many sons, the heirs of salvation. They are the peculiar theme of the whole chapter. Anyone following the apostle's reasoning would naturally understand this expression to refer to them. It is straining it to refer it to any others. If it does refer to others, it might as well refer to angels (much more naturally so than of the world); for he is speaking of them, not of the world at all. The fifteenth chapter of 1 Cor.is an illustration of this.The apostle is treating of the resurrection of the saints, not of the wicked. It is only by keeping this in view that his statement there regarding the *"all"* can be fully understood. So the *"each"* here referred to must be the *"each"* of those he was speaking of. And the singular used here is very striking, not simply the individualizing the saints, but as doing so in connection with the whole work of Christ. All that Christ did, He did for each! – His whole work, His whole propitiation, His whole tasting of death belongs to each, just as much as if only one had been saved. The whole of what Christ did is the property of each saint. His work is not made up of so many parts, or extending to certain dimensions (greater or smaller according to the number of the saved) so that each of them gets a part of Himself and a part of His work. No, His work is such that each gets the whole of it – the whole of His glorious self, the whole of His glorious work. Each gets the benefit of His tasting death, as if endured for himself singly, alone.

Only a few hints have been thrown out to lead you, to establish you in the faith, to repel the objections of opponents. The real question before us is this, Was the atonement of Christ a definite or an indefinite thing? That is the essence and marrow of the controversy. It is upon this that the case of things hinges. There is a mighty difference between a definite and an indefinite work. Search the Scriptures and see if the language in which they speak does not necessarily imply something definite and certain – something which infalliby secured the object for which the Son of God took flesh and died, (which was, as you know, *"to bring many sons to glory"*).

*"For the transgression of My people was He stricken"* (Isa. 53:8). *"The church which He has purchased with His own blood"* (Acts 20:29).

## 7. FAITH AND THE GOSPEL

*"For by grace you are saved through faith, and that not of yourselves, it is the gift of God"* (Ephesians 2:8,9).

*"Being justified by faith, we have peace with God"* (Rom. 5:1).

Scripture presents faith to us in more aspects than one. It is sometimes called hearing, sometimes knowing, sometimes believing, or receiving, or trusting. Strictly speaking, it is simply the belief of the truth, yet it is referred to throughout Scripture under these different names. These may be said to be its different stages, and it is useful oftentimes to lay hold of it at each of these and contemplate it under each of these views. They are not in reality the same thing, yet they illustrate the same thing, they point to one object. The things we hear, the truth we know, the tidings we believe, the gift we receive, the Being we trust may be different in one sense – yet in another they are the same.

Some adopt one aspect exclusively, some another, so that the object itself is lost sight of. Some particular definition is fastened on and elevated to such prominence as to become little better than a party watchword (furnishing much matter for self-righteous pride and confidence).

One person glories in what he calls his simple views of faith, spurning every other idea of it but what he calls 'the bare belief of the bare truth.' Ask such, "Where is your child-like confidence in God, where is the resting of your soul upon Jesus Himself as the resting place? You are making a saviour of your faith, an idol of the truth. You are just as self-righteous and proud in your 'simple views of faith' as is the mystic whose religion you profess to shun. Your God seems to be a mere bundle of abstract propositions; your Saviour a mere collection of evangelical phrases, which you use as the shibboleth of a sect."

Another goes to the opposite extreme overlooking the simplicity of faith. He under-values the truth. He is wholly occupied with some mystical actions of his own mind, trying to exert himself to put forth some indescribable efforts which he calls 'receiving and resting on Christ.' Say to such, "You are on the road to mysticism. You are occupied with your own self, with your own actions and feelings. You are making a Saviour of them. You certainly need more simple views of true faith. You need to be called down from self-righteous perplexities about your own acts, to the precious word of truth which you are despising, as if it contained no comfort for you unless you are conscious of connecting certain acts of your own to it."

From this you will see how it is quite possible to admit the full meaning of those words in Scripture which speak of confidence, and trust, and rest, etc.; while, at the same time, we rejoice in those other expressions which represent faith as an "acknowledgment of the truth," and the salvation of the sinner as the result of his "coming to the knowledge of the truth." It is quite consistent with Scripture to represent peace as flowing from confidence in God through Christ, and yet as rising from "believing the record which God has given of His Son."

Without attempting to give a definition of faith, let me say in a few words that any faith which goes no farther than the intellect can neither save nor sanctify. It is no faith at all. It is unbelief. No faith is saving except that which links us to the person of a loving Saviour. Whatever falls short of this is not faith in Christ. So, while salvation is described sometimes in Scripture as a *"coming to the knowledge of the truth,"* it is more commonly represented as a *"coming to Christ Himself." "You will not come to Me that you might have life"; "Him that comes to Me I will not cast out."*

But whatever view of faith we take, one thing is obvious; that it is from first to last *"the gift of God."* Make it as simple as you please, still it is the result of the Holy Spirit's direct, immediate, all-quickening power. Never attempt to make faith simple, with the view of getting rid of the Spirit to produce it. This is one of the most wretched devices of Satan in the present evil day. By all means correct every mistake in regard to faith, by which hindrances are thrown in the sinner's way, or darkness thrown around the soul. Show him that it is the object of faith, even with Christ and His cross, that he has to do, not with his own actions of faith; that it is not virtue and merit that are in Christ Jesus alone. Tell him to look outward, not inward for his peace. Beat him off from his self-righteous efforts to get up a particular kind of faith or particular acts of faith in order to obtain something for himself – something short of Christ to rest upon. Simplify, explain and illustrate faith to such a one, but never imagine that you are going to make the Spirit's help less absolutely necessary.

This is what the aim of the propagators of the new theology seems to be. Their object in simplifying faith is to bring it within the reach of the unrenewed man, so that by performing this very simple act he may become a renewed man. In other words, their object is to make man the beginner of his own salvation. He takes the first step, and God does the rest! He believes, and then God comes in and saves him! This is nothing but a flat and bold denial of the Spirit's work altogether. If at any time more than another the sinner needs the Spirit's power, it is at the beginning. And he who denies the need of the Spirit at the beginning cannot believe in it at the after stages — nay, cannot believe in the need of the Spirit's work at all. The mightiest and most insuperable difficulty lies at the beginning. If the sinner can get over that without the Spirit, he will easily get over the rest. If he does not need Him to enable him to believe, he will not need Him to enable him to love. If when a true object is presented to me, I can believe without the Spirit, then when a lovable object is presented I can love without the Spirit. In short, what is there in the whole Christian life which I cannot do of myself, if I can begin this career without help from God? The denial of the Holy Spirit's direct agency, in faith and conversion, is the denial of His whole work in the souls both of the saint and the sinner.

But is it not said, *"Faith comes by hearing"*? Certainly. And who doubts the blessed truth? How can there be faith where there is not something to be believed? "There is an inseparable relation between faith and the Word, and these can no more be torn asunder from each other than rays of light from the sun" (John Calvin). But does this mean that hearing alone is necessary to the production of faith? The words in the original explain this, "Faith arises out of what we hear, and what we hear comes to us through means of the word of God." Who then would say anything but what the apostle does here?, viz., that the foundation of the truth is what we hear (literally, a hearing, or a report). But does this exclude the Spirit from His work in preparing the soul for believing what it hears?

Having said this much as to faith itself, let a few words be added as to what it receives, *"the glorious gospel of the blessed God."* That which we preach, and which faith believes, *"is the glad tidings of great joy."* It is God's testimony of His own character, His declaration of His gracious mind towards the sinner, the utterance of His manifold yearnings over His lost and long-wandered offspring. That which we make known is the story of Divine love. We tell men that there is such a thing as love in God towards the sinful; that this love has found vent to itself in a righteous way, and that all are welcome to the participation and enjoyment of this love. We show them how God has opened up His heart to let them see what riches of grace are there; and how He has done a work on the earth by which we may measure the infinite dimensions of that gracious heart. This is the good news we bring, the tidings we present to the sinner to be believed, to be rejoiced in with joy unspeakable and full of glory. And this gospel is free, truly, absolutely, unconditionally free. It is without money and without price, making known the exceeding riches of God's grace. This news shows us how these riches are pouring themselves freely upon all this fallen world. It shows that there is not only grace in God for sinners, but also that that grace has found vent to itself and is flowing down in a righteous channel to unrighteous man. It tells us that the darkness is past, that the true light has arisen upon the world. It tells us that the veil is torn from top to bottom, that every sinner may go freely in; that there is forgiving love in the bosom of the Father; that every sinner, without exception, is invited to avail himself of it. It points each wandering eye to the Cross, that it may read there the Divine compassion towards the rebellious, the unholy. The good news comes to every man, inviting him to partake of all the fullness of God.

"Shall we tell men that unless they are holy they must not believe on Jesus Christ; that they must not venture on Christ for salvation until they are qualified and fit to be received and welcomed by Him? This would be a forbearing to preach the gospel at all, or to forbid all men to come to Christ. He is well qualified to come to us, but a sinner out of Christ has no qualifications for Christ but sin and misery . . . Shall we tell people that they should not believe on Christ too soon? It is impossible that they should do it too soon. Can a man obey the command of the gospel too soon or do the work of God too soon? . . . If he should say, what is it to believe on Jesus Christ? As to this, I find no question in the word, but that all did some way understand the notion of it. They all, both Christ's enemies and disciples, knew that faith in Him was believing that the man, Jesus of Nazareth, was the Son of God, the Messiah and Saviour of the world, so as to receive and look for salvation in His name. If he still asks what he is to believe, you tell him that he is not called to believe in Christ, nor that his sins are pardoned, nor that his is a justified man — but he must believe God's record concerning Christ; and that this record is, that God gives to us eternal life in His Son, Jesus Christ, and that all who with the heart believe this report and rest their souls on these glad tidings shall be saved.

"If he still says that believing is hard, ask what it is that makes believing hard for him. Is it unwillingness to be saved? Is it a distrust of the truth of the Gospel? This he will not dare admit. Is it a doubt of Christ's ability or goodwill to save? This is to contradict the testimony of God in the Gospel . . . If he says that he cannot believe on Christ, and that a Divine power is needed to draw it forth, which he does not find within himself, you tell him that believing on Christ Jesus is not a work, but it is a resting on Jesus Christ; that this pretence is as miserable as if a man who was weary from his journey, who was not able to go one step farther, should begin to argue that he was so tired that he could not even lie down to rest — when in fact, he could neither stand nor go." (end quote of the great Scottish preacher, Robert Trail).

But I may be asked, How is all this freeness consistent with Christ's substitution for His church alone? I answer that the Gospel is not, "Christ died for the elect;" neither is it, "Christ died for all." But it is, "Christ died for sinners." It was thus that the apostles preached and that men believed. Any reader of the Acts of the Apostles can see this. They preached the glad tidings in such terms as these: *"To Him all the prophets give witness, that through His name whosoever believes in Him shall receive remission of sins"* (Acts 10:43). Or again, *"Be it known to you, men and brothers, that through this One the forgiveness of sins is preached to you. And by Him all who believe are justified from all things, from which you could not be justified by the law of Moses"* (13:38-39).

The passage in 1 Cor. 15:3 is often appealed to as a proof that the apostles preached everywhere that Christ died for all . . . We have a full account of their preaching in this book of Acts, and nothing of the sort is stated there. But, in regard to this passage, . . . how is it possible to extort such a declaration out of it? The Apostle went to Corinth. He stood up in a city of heathen. He cried out, *"Christ died for our sins."* He did not say, "Christ died for all and everyone;" no, he did not say, "for your sins;" he simply said, *"for our sins."* Now, not wishing to restrict the Gospel, nor to make it appear as if it were not literally and actually for all but noting that the words here are plainly restrictive, we might expect to hear some cavilling hearer in the way, like some modern objects, Oh! He does not preach the gospel. He says that Christ died for our sins, but he should have said that Christ died not only for our sins, but for the sins of all.

The man who lays stress on what he calls the gospel upon all, upon me, or on the other hand, upon the elect of the church plainly does not believe the gospel as the apostles did And the man who, in believing, is turning his whole thoughts to these words, is going aside from the tidings themselves. He is thinking of nothing but himself and the bearing of the Gospel upon himslef alone. He is losing sight of the glorious revelation of Himself, which God has made in the Gospel, and he is only concerned about that part of it which he thinks includes his own salvation.

But how is this? you will ask. For the obvious reason that it is not with the work of Christ as a work done especially for myself that I have to do with in the first place in believing. But first I must recognize it as a work which opens up to me the grace of God. It shows me that there is such a thing as grace, or free love to sinners. It is the pledge of its reality and the measure of its extent and dimensions. Whether we suppose it to be work done for many or few, still it is the declaration of God's free love, and it is that free love that is the sinner's resting-place. The real question that troubles an anxious soul is in substance this: "Is there free love in God, free love reaching even to the vilest? Does He have such a free love that no amount of sin can repel or quench? Is there enough of free love to reach even to me and to remedy a case like mine?" The work of Christ settles all these perplexities, and yet in settling them it does not raise the question, "Was the work done especially for me?" any more than it raises the question, "Am I elected, or not?" It is the meaning of that work to which an inquirer has to look in the first place, not to its ultimate and particular destination. He who understands the character of God as the Lord God who is merciful and gracious will not be disquieted by the subtle suggestion of the evil one to ask, Am I elected? So he who understands the work of Christ, which is the grand exposition and opening up of the character of God, will never think of putting the question, "Was that work especially intended for me?" Apart from such a question, that work contains enough to remove all his fears.

HORATIUS BONAR

# JONATHAN EDWARDS ON THE QUESTION,

## IS GOD THE AUTHOR OF SIN?

*Concerning that Objection against the Doctrine*
*which has been maintained, that it makes*
*God the Author of Sin.*

It is urged by *Arminians*, that the doctrine of the necessity of men's volitions, or their necessary connection with antecedent events and circumstances, makes the first cause, and supreme order of all things, the Author of Sin; in that he has so constituted the state and course of things, that sinful volitions become necessary, in consequence of his disposal. Dr. *Whitby*, in his Discourse on the Freedom of the Will, cites one of the ancients, as on his side, declaring that this opinion of the necessity of the will, "absolves sinners, as doing nothing of their own accord which was evil, and would cast all the blame of all the wickedness committed in the world upon God, and upon his Providence, if that were admitted by the assertors of this fate; whether he himself did necessitate them to do these things, or ordered matters so, that they should be constrained to do them by some other cause." And the doctor says, in another place, "In the nature of the thing, and in the opinion of philosophers, *causa deficiens, in rebus necessariis, ad causam per se efficientem reducenda est.* In things necessary, the deficient cause must be reduced to the efficient; and in this case the reason is evident; because the not doing what is required, or not avoiding what is forbidden, being a defect, must follow from the position of the necessary cause of that deficiency."

Concerning this, I would observe the following things: —

1. If there be any difficulty in this matter, it is nothing peculiar to this scheme; it is no difficulty or disadvantage, wherein it is distinguished from the scheme of *Arminians*; and, therefore, not reasonably objected by them.

Dr. Whitby supposes, that if sin necessarily follows from God's withholding assistance, or if that assistance be not given, which is absolutely necessary to the avoiding of evil, then, in the nature of the thing, God must be as properly the author of that evil, as if it were the efficient cause of it; from whence, according to what he himself says of the devils and damned spirits, God must be the proper author of their perfect unrestrained wickedness: he must be the efficient cause of the great pride of the devils, and of their perfect malignity against God, Christ, his saints, and all that is good, and of the insatiable cruelty of their disposition; for he allows that God has so forsaken them, and does so withhold his assistance from them, that they are incapacitated from doing good, and determined only to evil. Our doctrine, in its consequence, makes God the author of men's sins in this world, no more and in no other sense, than his doctrine, in its consequence, makes God the author of the hellish pride and malice of the Devils: and doubtless the latter is as odious an effect as the former.

Again: if it will follow at all that God is the author of sin, from what has been supposed of a sure and infallible connection between antecedents and consequents, it will *follow because of this, viz.* that for God to be author or orderer of those things which he knows before hand, will infallibly be attended with such a consequence, is the same thing, in effect, as for him to be the author of that consequence; but, if this be so, this is a difficulty which equally attends the doctrine of *Arminians* themselves; at least, of those of them who allow God's certain fore-knowledge of all events; for on the supposition of such a fore-knowledge, this is the case with respect to every sin that is committed; God knew, that if he ordered and brought to pass such and such events, such sins would infallibly follow. As for instance, God certainly foreknew, long before Judas was born, that if he ordered things so, that there should be such a man born, at such a time and at such a place, and that his life should be preserved, and that he should, in divine

32

Providence, be led into acquaintance with Jesus; and that his heart should be so influenced by God's spirit or providence, as to be inclined to be a follower of Christ; and that he should be one of those twelve, which should be chosen constantly to attend him as his family; and that his health should be preserved, so that he should go up to Jerusalem, at the last passover in Christ's life; and it should be so ordered, that Judas should see Christ's kind treatment of the woman which anointed him at Bethany, and have that reproof from Christ, which he had at that time, and see and hear other things which excited his enmity against his Master, and other circumstances should be ordered, as they were ordered; it would be what would most certainly and infallibly follow, that Judas would betray his Lord, and would soon after hang himself, and die impenitent, and be sent to hell for his horrid wickedness.

Therefore, this supposed difficulty ought not to be brought as an objection against the scheme which has been maintained, as disagreeing with the Arminian scheme, seeing it is no difficulty owing to such a disagreement; but a difficulty wherein the Arminians share with us. That must be unreasonably made an objection against our differing from them, which we should not escape or avoid at all by agreeing with them.

Therefore I would observe,

II. They who object, that this doctrine makes God the author of sin, ought distinctly to explain what they mean by that phrase *the author of sin*. I know the phrase, as it is commonly used, signifies something very ill. If by *the author of sin*, be meant *the sinner, the agent,* or *actor of sin,* or *the doer of a wicked thing*; so it would be a reproach and blasphemy, to suppose God to be the author of sin. In this sense, I utterly deny God to be the author of sin; rejecting such an imputation on the Most High, as what is infinitely to be abhorred; and deny any such thing to be the consequence of what I have laid down. But if, by *the author of sin,* is meant the permitter, or not a hinderer of sin; and, at the same time, a disposer of the state of events, in such a manner, for wise, holy, and most excellent ends and purposes, that sin, if it be permitted or not hindered, will most certainly and infallibly follow; I say, if this be all that is meant, by being the author of sin, I do not deny that God is the author of sin, (though I dislike and reject the phrase, as that which by use and custom is apt to carry another sense) it is no reproach for the Most High to be thus the author of sin. This is not to be the actor of sin, but, on the contrary, *of holiness.* What God doth herein is holy; and a glorious exercise of the infinite excellency of his nature; and, I do not deny, that God's being thus the author of sin, follows from what I have laid down; and, I assert, that it equally follows from the doctrine which is maintained by most of the Arminian divines.

That it is most certainly so, that God is in such a manner the disposer and orderer of sin, is evident, if any credit is to be given to the Scriptures; as well as because it is impossible, in the nature of things, to be otherwise. In such a manner God ordered the obstinacy of Pharaoh, in his refusing to obey God's commands, to let the people go. Exodus 4:21: "I will harden his heart, and he shall not let the people go." Chap. 7:2—5: "Aaron, thy brother shall speak unto Pharaoh, that he send the children of Israel out of his land. And I will harden Pharaoh's heart, and multiply my signs and my wonders in the land of Egypt. But Pharaoh shall not hearken unto you; that I may lay mine hand upon Egypt, by great judgments," etc. Chap. 9:12: "And the Lord hardened the heart of Pharaoh, and he hearkened not unto them, as the Lord had spoken unto Moses." Chap. 10:1,2: "And the Lord said unto Moses, Go in unto Pharaoh; for I have hardened his heart, and the heart of his servants, that I might shew these my signs before him, and that thou mayest tell it in the ears of thy son, and thy son's son, what thing I have wrought in Egypt, and my signs which I have done amongst them, that ye may know that I am the Lord." Chap. 14:4: "And I will harden Pharaoh's heart, that he shall follow after them; and I will be honoured upon Pharaoh, and upon all his host." Ver. 8: "And the Lord hardened the heart of Pharaoh king of Egypt, and he pursued after the children of Israel." And it is certain, that in such a manner God, for wise and good ends, ordered that event, Joseph being sold into Egypt by his brethren. Gen. 45:5: "Now, therefore, be not grieved, nor angry with yourselves, that ye sold me hither; for God did send me before you to preserve life." Ver. 7,8: "God did send me before you to preserve a posterity in the earth, and to save your lives by a great deliverance: so that now it was not you that sent me hither, but God." Psalms 107:17: "He sent a man before them, even Joseph, who was sold for a servant." It is certain, that thus God ordered the sin and folly of Sihon, king of the Amorites, in refusing, to let the people of Israel pass by him peaceably. Deut. 2:30: "But Sihon, king of Heshbon, would not let us pass by him; for the Lord thy God hardened his spirit, and made his heart obstinate, that he might deliver him into thine hand." It is certain, that God thus ordered the sin and folly of the kings of Canaan, that they attempted not to make peace with Israel, but, with a stupid boldness and obstinacy, set themselves violently to oppose them and their God. Josh. 11:20: "For it was of the Lord to harden their hearts, that they should come against Israel in battle, that he might destroy them utterly, and that they might have no favour; but that he might destroy them, as the Lord commanded Moses." It is evident, that thus God ordered the treacherous rebellion of Zedekiah against the king of Babylon, Jer. 52:3; "For through the anger of the Lord it came to pass in Jerusalem and Judah, until he had cast them out from his presence, that Zedekiah rebelled against the king of Babylon." So 2 Kings 24:20. And it is exceeding manifest, that God thus ordered the rapine and unrighteous ravages of Nebuchadnezzar, in spoiling and ruining the nations round about. Jer. 25:9: "Behold, I will send and take all the families of the north, saith the Lord, and Nebuchadnezzar my servant, and will bring them against this land, and against all the nations round about; and will utterly destroy them, and make them an astonishment, and an hissing, and perpetual desolations." Chap. 43:10,11; "I will send and take Nebuchadnezzar, the king of Babylon, my servant; and I will set his throne upon these stones that I have hid, and he shall spread his royal pavilion over them. And when he cometh, he shall smite the land of Egypt, and deliver such as are for death to death, and such as are for captivity to captivity, and such as are for the sword to the sword." Thus God represents himself as sending for Nebuchadnezzar, and taking of him and his armies, and bringing him against the nations, which were to be destroyed by him, to that very end, that he might utterly destroy them, and make them desolate; and as appointing the work that he should do, so particularly, that the very persons were designed, that he should kill with the sword; and those that should be killed with famine and pestilence, and those that should be carried into captivity; and that in doing all these things, he should act as his servant; by which, less cannot be intended, than that he should serve his purposes and designs. And in Jer. 27:4,5,6, God declares, how he would cause him thus to serve his designs, viz. by bringing this to pass in his sovereign disposals, as the great Possessor and Governor of the Universe, that disposes all things just as pleases him. "Thus saith the Lord of Hosts, the God of Israel; I have made the earth, the man, and the beast, that are upon the ground, by my great power, and my stretched out arm; and have given it unto whom it seemed meet unto me; and now I have given all these lands into the hands of Nebuchadnezzar MY SERVANT, and the beasts of the field have I given also to serve him." And Nebuchadnezzar is spoken of as doing these things, by having his *arms strengthened* by God, and having *God's sword put into his hands, for this end.* Ezek. 30:24,25,26. Yea, God speaks of his terribly ravaging and wasting the nations, and cruelly destroying all sorts, without distinction of sex or age, as the weapon in God's hand, and the instrument of his indignation, which God makes use of to fulfil his own purposes, and execute his own vengeance. Jer. 51:20, etc. "Thou art my battle-axe, and weapons of war. For with thee will I break in pieces the nations, and with thee I will destroy kingdoms, and with thee I will break in pieces the horse and his rider, and with thee I will break in pieces the chariot and his rider; with thee also will I break in pieces man and woman; and with thee will I break in pieces old and young; and with thee will I break in pieces the young man and the maid," etc. It is represented, that the designs of Nebuchadnezzar, and those that destroyed Jerusalem, never could have been accomplished, had not God determined them, as well as they. Lam. 3:37: "Who is he that saith,and it cometh to pass, and the

Lord commanded it not?" And yet the king of Babylon's thus destroying the nations, and especially the Jews, is spoken of as his great wickedness, for which God finally destroyed him. Isa. 14:4,5,6,12; Hab. 2:5—12; and Jer. 50 and 51. It is most manifest, that God, to serve his own designs, providentially ordered Shimei's cursing David. 2 Sam. 16:10,11: "The Lord hath said unto him, curse David — Let him curse, for the Lord hath bidden him."

It is certain that God thus, for excellent, holy, gracious, and glorious ends, ordered the fact which they committed, who were concerned in Christ's death; and that therein they did but fulfil God's designs. As, I trust, no Christian will deny, it was the design of God that Christ should *be crucified*, and that for this end he came into the world. It is very manifest, by many Scriptures, that the whole affair of Christ's crucifixion, with its circumstances, and the treachery of *Judas*, that made way for it, was ordered in God's providence, in pursuance of his purpose; notwithstanding the violence that is used with those plain Scriptures, to obscure and pervert the sense of them. Acts 2:23: "Him being delivered, by the determinate counsel and fore-knowledge of God, ye have taken, and with wicked hands, have crucified and slain." Luke 22:21,22: "But behold the hand of him that betrayeth me, is with me on the table; and truly the Son of man goeth, as it was determined." Acts 4:27,28: "For of a truth, against the holy child Jesus, whom thou hast anointed, both Herod and Pontius Pilate, with the Gentiles, and the people of Israel, were gathered together, for to do whatsoever thy hand and thy counsel determined before to be done." Acts 3:17,18: "And now, brethren, I wot that through ignorance ye did it, as did also your rulers; but these things, which God before had shewed by the mouth of all his prophets, that Christ should suffer, he hath so fulfilled." So that what these murderers of Christ did, is spoken of as what God brought to pass or ordered, and that by which he fulfilled his own word.

In Rev. 17:17, "The agreeing of the kings of the earth to give their kingdom to the beast, though it was a very wicked thing in them, is spoken of as *a fulfilling God's will*, and what *God hath put into their hearts to do*." It is manifest that God sometimes permits sin to be committed, and at the same time orders things so, that if he permits the fact, it will come to pass, because on some accounts, he sees it needful and of importance, that it should come to pass. Matt. 18:7: "It must needs be, that offences come; but woe to that man by whom the offence cometh." With 1 Cor. 11:19, "For there must also be heresies among you, that they which are approved may be made manifest among you."

Thus it is certain and demonstrable, from the holy Scriptures, as well as the nature of things, and the principles of *Arminians*, that God permits sin; and at the same time, so orders things, in his Providence, that it certainly and infallibly will come to pass, in consequence of his permission.

I proceed to observe in the next place,

III. That there is a great difference between God's being concerned thus, by his permission, in an event and act, which, in the inherent subject and agent of it, is sin (though the event will certainly follow on his permission) and his being concerned in it by *producing* it and exerting the act of sin; or between his being the *order* of its certain existence, by *not hindering* it, under certain circumstances, and his being the proper *actor or author* of it, by a *positive agency or efficiency*. And this notwithstanding what Dr. *Whitby* offers about a saying of philosophers, that *causa deficiens in rebus necessariis, ad causam per se efficientem reducenda est*. As there is a vast difference between the sun's being the cause of the lightsomeness and warmth of the atmosphere, and brightness of gold and diamonds, by its presence and positive influence; and its being the occasion of darkness and frost in the night, by its motion, whereby it descends below the horizon. The motion of the sun is the occasion of the latter kind of events; but it is not the proper cause, efficient or producer of them; though they are necessarily consequent on that motion, under such circumstances; no more is any action of the divine Being the cause of the evil of men's wills. If the sun were the proper *cause* of cold and darkness, it would be the *fountain* of these things, as it is the fountain of light and heat, and then something might be argued from the nature of cold and darkness, to a likeness of nature in the sun; and it might be justly inferred, that the sun itself is dark and cold, and that his beams are black and frosty. But from its being the cause no otherwise than by its departure, no such thing can be inferred, but the contrary; it may justly be argued, that the sun is a bright and hot body, if cold and darkness are found to be the consequence of its withdrawment; and the more constantly and necessarily these effects are connected with, and confined to its absence, the more strongly does it argue the sun to be the fountain of light and heat. So, inasmuch as sin is not the fruit of any positive agency or influence of the Most High, but, on the contrary, arises from the withholding of his action and energy, and, under certain circumstances, necessarily follows on the want of his influence; this is no argument that he is sinful, or his operation evil, or has any thing of the nature of evil; but, on the contrary, that he, and his agency, are altogether good and holy, and that He is the Fountain of all holiness. It would be strange arguing, indeed, because men never commit sin, but only when God leaves them *to themselves,* and necessarily sin, when he does so, and therefore their sin is not *from themselves,* but from God; and so, that God must be a sinful Being; as strange as it would be to argue, because it is always dark when the sun is gone, and never dark when the sun is present, that therefore all darkness is from the sun, and that his disk and beams needs be black.

IV. It properly belongs to the Supreme and Absolute Governor of the Universe, to order all important events within his dominion, by his wisdom; but the events in the moral world are of the most important kind; such as the moral actions of intelligent creatures, and their consequences.

These events will be ordered by something. They will either be disposed by wisdom, or they will be disposed by change; that is, they will be disposed by blind and undesigning causes, if that were possible, and could be called a disposal. Is it not better, that the good and evil which happens in God's world, should be ordered, regulated, bounded, and determined by the good pleasure of an infinitely wise Being, who perfectly comprehends within his understanding and constant view, the universality of things, in all their extent and duration, and sees all the influence of every event, with respect to every individual thing and circumstance, throughout the grand system, and the whole of the eternal series of consequences; than to leave these things to fall out by chance, and to be determined by those causes which have no understanding or aim? Doubtless, in these important events, there is a better and a worse, as to the time, subject, place, manner, and circumstances of their coming to pass, with regard to their influence on the state and course of things; and if there be, it is certainly best that they should be determined to that time, place, etc. which is best; and therefore it is in its own nature fit, that wisdom, and not chance, should order these things. So that it belongs to the Being who is the possessor of infinite wisdom, and is the Creator and Owner of the whole system of created existences, and has the care of all; I say, it belongs to him, to take care of this matter; and he would not do what is proper for him, if he should neglect it; and it is so far from being unholy in him to undertake this affair, that it would rather have been unholy to neglect it; as it would have been a neglecting what fitly appertains to him; and so it would have been a very unfit and unsuitable neglect.

Therefore, the sovereignty of God doubtless extends to this matter; especially considering that if it should be supposed to be otherwise, and God should leave men's volitions, and all moral events, to the determination and disposition of blind unmeaning causes, or they should be left to happen perfectly without a cause; this would be no more consistent with liberty, in any notion of it, and particularly not in the *Arminian* notion of it, than if these events were subject to the disposal of divine Providence, and the will of man were determined by circumstances which are ordered and disposed by divine wisdom; as appears by what has already been observed; but it is evident, that such a providential disposing and determining men's moral actions, though it infers a moral necessity of those actions, yet it does not in the least infringe the real liberty of mankind; the only liberty that common sense teaches to be necessary to moral agency, which, as has been demonstrated, is not inconsistent with such necessity.

On the whole, it is manifest, that God may be, in the manner which has been described, the order and disposer of that event, which, in the inherent subject and agent, is moral evil; and yet his so doing may be no moral evil. He may will the disposal of such an event, and its coming to pass for good ends, and his will not be an immoral or sinful will, but a perfect holy will; and he may actually, in his providence, so dispose and permit things, that the event may be certainly and infallibly connected with such disposal and permission, and his act therein not be an immoral or unholy, but a perfect holy act. Sin may be an evil thing, and yet that there should be such a disposal and permission, as that it should come to pass, may be a good thing. This is no contradiction or inconsistence. Joseph's brethren selling him into Egypt, considered it only as it was acted by them, and with respect to their views and aims which were evil, was a very bad thing; but it was a good thing, as it was an event of God's ordering, and considered with respect to his views and aims which were good. Gen. 50:20: "As for you, ye thought evil against me; but God meant it unto good." So the crucifixion of Christ, if we consider only those things which belong to the event as it proceeded from his murderers, and are comprehended within the compass of the affair considered as their act, their principles, dispositions, views, and aims; so it was one of the most heinous things that ever was done; in many respects the most horrid of all acts; but consider it, as it was willed and ordered of God, in the extent of his designs and views, it was the most admirable and glorious of all events; and God's willing the event was the most holy volition of God, that ever was made known to men; and God's act in ordering it, was a divine act, which, above all others, manifests the moral excellency of the divine Being.

The consideration of these things may help us to a sufficient answer to the cavils of *Arminians,* concerning what has been supposed by many *Calvinists*; of a distinction between a *secret* and *revealed* will of God, and their diversity one from the other; supposing that the *Calvinists* herein ascribe inconsistent wills to the Most High; which is without any foundation. God's *secret* and *revealed* will, or, in other words, his *disposing* and *perceptive* will may be diverse, and exercised in dissimilar acts; the one in disapproving and opposing, the other in willing and determining, without any inconsistence. Because, although these dissimilar exercises of the divine will may, in some respects, relate to the same things, yet in strictness they have different and contrary objects, the one evil and the other good. Thus, for instance, the crucifixion of Christ was a thing contrary to the revealed or perceptive will of God; because, as it was viewed and done by his malignant murderers, it was a thing infinitely contrary to the holy nature of God, and so necessarily contrary to the holy inclination of his heart revealed in his law. Yet this does not at all hinder but that the crucifixion of Christ, considered with all those glorious consequences, which were within the view of the divine Omnisicence, might be indeed, and therefore might appear to God to be a glorious event; and consequently be agreeable to his will, though his will may be secret, *i.e.* not revealed in God's law; and thus considered, the crucifixion of Christ was not evil but good. If the secret exercises of God's will were of a kind that is dissimilar, and contrary to his revealed will, respecting the same, or like objects; if the objects of both were good or both evil; then, indeed to ascribe contrary kinds of volition or inclination to God, respecting these objects, would be to ascribe an inconsistent will to God; but to ascribe to Him different and opposite exercises of heart, respecting different objects, and objects contrary one to another, is so far from supposing God's will to be *inconsistent* with itself, that it cannot be supposed *consistent* with itself any other way; for any being to have a will of choice respecting good, and, at the same time, a will of rejection and refusal respecting evil, is to be very consistent; but the contrary, *viz.* to have the same will towards these contrary objects, and to choose and love both good and evil, at the same time, is to be very inconsistent.

There is no inconsistence in supposing, that God may hate a thing as it is in itself, and considered simply as evil, and yet that it may be his will it should come to pass, considering all consequences. I believe, there is no person of good understanding, who will venture to say, he is certain that it is impossible it should be best, taking in the whole compass and extent of existence, and all consequences in the endless series of events, that there should be such a thing as moral evil in the world. And, if so, it will certainly follow, that an infinitely wise Being, who always chooses what is best, must choose that there should be such a thing; and, if so, then such a choice is not an evil, but a wise and holy choice; and if so, then that providence which is agreeable to such a choice, is a wise and holy providence. – Men do will sin as sin, and so are the authors and actors of it; they love it as sin, and for evil ends and purposes. God does not will sin as sin, or for the sake of any thing evil; though it be his pleasure so to order things, that He permitting sin will come to pass; for the sake of the great good that by his disposal shall be the consequence. His willing to order things so that evil should come to pass, for the sake of the contrary good, is no argument that He does not hate evil, as evil; and if so, then it is no reason why he may not reasonably forbid evil as evil, and punish it as such.

The *Arminians* themselves must be obliged, whether they will or no, to allow a distinction of God's will, amounting to just the same thing that *Calvinists* intend by their distinction of a *secret and revealed will*. They must allow a distinction of those things which God thinks best should be, considering all circumstances and consequences, and so are agreeable to his disposing will, and those things which he loves, and are agreeable to his nature, in themselves considered. Who is there that will dare to say, That the hellish pride, malice, and cruelty of devils are agreeable to God, and what he likes and approves? And yet, I trust, there is no Christian divine but what will allow, that it is agreeable to God's will so to order and dispose things concerning them, so to leave them to themselves, and give them up to their own wickedness, that this perfect wickedness should be a necessary consequence. Be sure Dr. *Whitby's* words do plainly suppose and allow it.

These following things may be laid down as maxims of plain truth, and indisputable evidence: –

1. That God is a *perfectly happy* Being, in the most absolute highest sense possible.

2. That it will follow from hence, that God is free from every thing that is *contrary to happiness*; and so, that in strict propriety of speech, there is no such thing as any pain, grief, or trouble in God.

3. When any intelligent being is really crossed and disappointed, and things are contrary to what he truly desires, he is the *less pleased*, or has less *pleasure*, his *pleasure* and *happiness is diminished*, and he suffers what is disagreeable to him, or is the subject of something that is of a nature contrary to joy and happiness, even pain and grief.

From this last axiom, it follows, that if no distinction is to be admitted between God's hatred of sin, and his will with respect to the event and the existence of sin, as the all-wise Determiner of all events, under the view of all consequences through the whole compass and series of things; I say, then it certainly follows, that the coming to pass of every individual act of sin is truly, all things being considered, contrary to his will, and that his will is really crossed in it; and this in proportion as He hates it; and as God's hatred of sin is infinite, by reason of the infinite contrariety of his holy nature to sin; so his will is infinitely crossed in every act of sin that happens; which is as much as to say, He endures that which is infinitely disagreeable to Him, by means of every act of sin that He sees committed; and, therefore, as appears by the preceding positions, He endures, truly and really, infinite grief or pain from every sin; and so He must be infinitely crossed, and suffer infinite pain every day, in millions and millions of instances; He must continually be the subject of an immense number of real, and truly infinitely great crosses and vexations; which would be to make him infinitely the most miserable of all Beings.

If any objector should say, All that these things amount to is, that God *may do evil that good may come*; which is justly esteemed immoral and sinful in men; and therefore may be justly esteemed inconsistent with the moral perfections of God. I answer, That for God to dispose and permit evil, in the manner that has been spoken of, is not to do evil that good may come; for it is not to do evil at all. – In order to a thing's being morally evil, there must be one of these things belonging to it. Either it must be a thing *unfit* and *unsuitable* in its own nature; or it must have had a *bad tendency*; or it must proceed from an *evil disposition*, and be done for an evil end. But neither of these things can be attributed to God's ordering and permitting such events, as the immoral acts of creatures, for good ends. (1.) It is not *unfit in its own nature*, that He should do so; for it is in its own nature *fit*, that *infinite wisdom*, and not blind chance, should dispose moral good and evil in the world; and it is *fit*, that the Being who has *infinite wisdom*, and is the Maker, Owner, and Supreme Governor of the World, should take care of that matter; and therefore, there is no *unfitness* nor unsuitableness in his doing it. It may be unfit, and so immoral, for any other being to go about to order this affair; because they are not possessed of a wisdom, that in any manner fits them for it; and, in any other respects, they are not fit to be trusted with this affair; nor does it belong to them, they not being the owners and lords of the universe.

We need not be afraid to affirm, that if a wise and good man knew, with absolute certainty, it would be best, all things considered, that there should be such a thing as moral evil in the world, it would not be contrary to his wisdom and goodness for him to choose that it should be so. It is no evil desire to desire good, and to desire that which, all things considered, is best; and it is no unwise choice to choose that *that* should be, which is best should be; and to choose the existence of that being concerning which this is known, *viz.* that it is best it should be, and so is known in the whole to be most worthy to be chosen. On the contrary, it would be a plain defect in wisdom and goodness for him not to choose it; and the reason why he might not order it, if he were able, would not be because he might not desire it, but only the ordering of that matter does not belong to him. But it is no harm for Him who is, by right, and in the greatest propriety, the Supreme Orderer of all things, to order every thing in such a manner, as it would be a point of wisdom in Him to choose that they should be ordered. If it would be a plain defect of wisdom and goodness in a Being, not to choose that that should be, which He certainly knows it would, all things considered, be best should be (as was but now observed) then it must be impossible for a Being who has no defect of wisdom and goodness, to do otherwise than choose it should be; and that, for this very reason, because He is perfectly wise and good; and if it be agreeable to perfect wisdom and goodness for him to choose that it should be, and the ordering of all things supremely and perfectly belongs to him, it must be agreeable to infinite wisdom and goodness to order that it should be. If the choice is good, the ordering and disposing things according to that choice must also be good. It can be no harm in one to whom it belongs *to do his will in the armies of heaven, and amongst the inhabitants of the earth*, to execute a good volition. If this will be good, and the object of his will be, all things considered, good and best, then the choosing or willing it is not willing evil that good may come; and if so, then his ordering, according to that will is not doing evil, that good may come.

2. It is not of a bad tendency, for the Supreme Being thus to order and permit that moral evil to be, which is best should come to pass; for that it is of good tendency, is the very thing supposed in the point now in question. — Christ's crucifixion, though a most horrid act in them that perpetrated it, was of most glorious tendency as permitted and ordered of God.

3. Nor is there any need of supposing, it proceeds from any evil disposition or aim; for by the supposition, what is aimed at is good, and good is the actual issue, in the final result of things.

# Free-Will, A Slave!

*"And you are not willing to come to Me so that you may have life"*—
John 5:40, KJIIV

This is one of the great guns of the Arminians, mounted on the top of their walls, and often discharged with terrible noise against the poor Christians called Calvinists. I intend to spike the gun this morning; or, rather, to turn it on the enemy, for it was never theirs; this verse was never cast at their foundry at all. It was intended to teach the very opposite doctrine to that which they assert.

Usually, when the text is taken, the divisions are these: (1) Man has a will; (2) He is entirely free; (3) Men must make themselves willing to come to Christ, otherwise they will not be saved. Now, we shall have no such divisions. But we will endeavor to take a more calm look at the text; and not, because there happen to be the words 'will,' or 'will not' in it, run away with the conclusion that it teaches the doctrine of free-will.

### FREE-WILL IS SIMPLY RIDICULOUS

Free-will is nonsense. Freedom cannot belong to will any more than ponderability can belong to electricity. They are altogether different things. Free agency we may believe in, but free-will is simply ridiculous. The will is well known by all to be directed by the understanding, to be moved by motives, to be guided by other parts of the soul, and to be a secondary thing.

Philosophy and religion both discard at once the very thought of free-will. And I will go as far as Martin Luther, in that strong assertion of his, where he says, "If any man ascribes any of salvation, even the very least, to the free-will of man, he knows nothing of grace, and he has not learned Jesus Christ aright." It may seem a harsh sentiment, but he who in his soul believes that man does of his own free-will turn to God, cannot have been taught of God, for that is one of the first principles taught us that we of ourselves have neither will nor power, but that He gives both, that He is the *Alpha and Omega* [the beginning and the end] in the salvation of men.

### FOUR POINTS ON THIS TEXT

1. Every man is dead, because it is written, *"You are not willing to come to Me that you may have LIFE."*

2. There is life in Jesus Christ, *"You are not willing to come to ME that you may have life."*

3. There is life in Christ Jesus for everyone that comes for it, *"You are not willing to come to Me that you may have life;"* implying that all who go WILL have life.

40

4. The gist of the text lies here, that no man by nature ever will come to Christ, for the text says, *"You are NOT willing to come to Me that you may have life."* So far from asserting that men of their own wills ever do such a thing, it boldly and flatly denies it, saying, *"You ARE NOT WILLING to come to Me that you may have life."* Why, beloved, I am almost ready to exclaim, Have all free-willers no knowledge that they dare to run in the teeth of inspiration? Have all those that deny the doctrine of grace no sense? Have they so departed from God that they wrest this to prove free-will; whereas the text plainly says, *"You ARE NOT WILLING to come to Me that you may have life."*

## THERE IS NO LIFE IN DEATH

First, then, our text implies that men by nature are dead. No being needs to go after life if he has life in himself. The text speaks very strongly when it says, *"You are not willing to come to Me that you may have life,"* though it does not say it in words, yet it does in effect affirm that men need a life more than they have themselves. My hearers, we are all dead unless we have been begotten to a lively hope.

## LEGALLY DEAD AND CONDEMNED

All of us by nature are legally dead: *"In the day you eat of it you shall die the death,"* said God to Adam. And though Adam did not die in that moment naturally, he died legally; that is to say, death was recorded against him. At the Old Bailey, as soon as the judge puts on the black cap and pronounces the sentence, the man is reckoned to be dead at law. Though perhaps a month may intervene before he is brought on the scaffold to endure the sentence of the law, yet the law looks on him as a dead man. It is impossible for him to transact anything. He cannot inherit, he cannot bequeath; he is nothing – he is a dead man. The country considers him as not being alive in it at all. There is an election – he is not asked for his vote because he is considered to be dead. He is shut up in his condemned cell and he is dead. Ah! You ungodly sinners who have never had life in Christ, you are alive this morning by reprieve, but know this, that you are legally dead. God considers you as being dead, for in that day when your father Adam touched the forbidden fruit, and when you yourself sinned, God, the Eternal Judge, put on the black cap, as it were, and condemned you. You talk mightily of your own standing and goodness and morality, but where is it? Scripture says, *"You are condemned already."* You are not to wait to be condemned at the judgement day – that will be the execution of the sentence: *"You are condemned already!"* In the moment you sinned, your names were all written in the black book of justice; everyone was then sentenced by God to death, unless he found a substitute in the person of Christ for his sins.

What would you think if you were to go into the Old Bailey Prison and see the condemned culprit sitting in his cell laughing and merry? You would say, The man is a fool, for he is condemned and is to be executed, yet look how merry he is. Ah! And how foolish is the worldly man: While sentence of death is recorded against him, he lives in merriment and mirth! Do you think the sentence of God is of no effect? Is it true that your sin which is written with an iron pen on the rocks forever has no horrors in it? God has said that you are already condemned. If you would only feel this, it would mingle bitter tears in your sweet cups of joy. Your dances would cease and your laughter would be quenched in sighing. If we would lay it to our soul that by nature we have no life in God's sight, we would all weep. We are condemned: death is actually and positively recorded against us. In God's sight we are even now in ourselves considered dead, as much so as if we had already actually been cast into hell. We are condemned by our sin. We do not yet suffer the final penalty of it, but it is written against us — we are legally dead, and we cannot find life unless we find legal life in the person of Christ.

## NOT ONLY LEGALLY DEAD, BUT WE ARE SPIRITUALLY DEAD

Besides being legally dead, we are also spiritually dead. For not only did the sentence pass in the book, but it passed in the heart; it entered the conscience, it operated on the soul, on the judgment, on the imagination, on everything. *"In the day you eat of it, you shall surely die"* was not only fulfilled by the sentence recorded, but by something that took place within Adam. In a certain moment this body will die — the blood will stop, the pulse will cease, the breath will no longer fill the lungs — in the same way, the day Adam ate that fruit, his soul died: his imagination lost its mighty power to climb into celestial things and see Heaven; his will lost its power always to choose that which is good; his judgment lost all ability to tell right from wrong with certainty (though something was retained in conscience); his memory became tainted, liable to hold evil things and let righteous things glide away; every one of his powers ceased to have moral vitality. Goodness had been the vitality of his powers, and that departed. Virtue, holiness, integrity, these, among others, were the life of the man. When these departed from man , he was dead. And now so far as spiritual things are concerned, every man is *"dead in trespasses and sins."* Nor is the soul less dead in a carnal man than the body is when it is committed to the grave. It is actually and positively dead. It is not by a metaphor, for Paul does not speak in a metaphor when he affirms, *"even when we were dead in sins, He made us alive together with Christ"* (Ephesians 2:5).

O how I desire to preach to your hearts concerning this subject! It was bad enough when I described death as having been recorded. But now I speak of it as having actually taken place in your hearts. You are not what you once were — you are not what you were in Adam, not what you were when you were created. Man was made pure and holy. You are not the perfect creatures of which some boast. You are altogether fallen, you have gone out of the way, you have become corrupt and filthy (Romans 3:10-17). O, do not listen to the siren song of those who tell you of your moral dignity, those who tell you of your mighty elevation in matters of salvation. You are not perfect, but that great word 'ruin' is written on your heart; death is stamped on your spirit.

Do not conceive, O man of morality, that you will be able to stand before God in your morality, for you are nothing but a carcase embalmed in legality. You are a corpse arrayed in some fine robes, but you are still corrupt in God's sight. And do not think, you who possess natural religion, that you may by your own might and power make yourself acceptable to God. Why, man, you are dead! And you may dress up the dead as gloriously as you please, but you still would be participating in a solemn mockery. Look upon queen Cleopatra, put the crown on her head, decorate her in her royal robes, let her sit in state — when you've done it all, will a cold chill not run through you when you pass by her hollow mummy? She is beautiful, even now in her death — but how horrible it is to stand by the side of even a dead queen, one celebrated for her majestic beauty! So you may be glorious in your beauty, fair and amiable and lovely; you may put the crown of honesty on your head and wear all the garments of uprightness, but unless God has made you alive, O man, unless the Spirit has had dealings with your soul, you are in God's sight as obnoxious as the chilly corpse is to yourself! You would not choose to live with a corpse sitting at your table. God does not love your being in His sight when your are dead. He is angry with you every day while you are in sin, for you are in death when you are still in your sins. O believe this, take it to your soul, appropriate it, for it is most true that you are dead, spiritually as well as legally.

ETERNAL DEATH The third kind of death is the consummation of the other two. It is eternal death. It is the execution of the legal sentence; it is the consummation of the spiritual death. Eternal death is the death of the soul. It takes place after the body has been laid in the grave, after the soul has departed from it. If legal death is terrible, it is because of its consequences. And if spiritual death is dreadful, it is because of that which shall come after it. The two deaths of which we have spoken are the roots, and that death which is to come is the flower of it.

O that I had words that I might draw the picture of eternal death to you! The soul has come before its Maker; the Book has been opened; the sentence has been uttered, *"Depart from Me, cursed ones!"* The universe has been shaken and the very spheres dim with the frown of the Creator. The soul has departed to the depths where it is to dwell with others in eternal death. O how horrible is its position now! Its bed is a bed of flame; the sights it sees are murdering ones that frighten its spirit; the sounds it hears are shrieks, and wails, and moans, and groans. All that the body knows is the infliction of miserable pain! It has the possession of unutterable woe, of unmitigated misery. The soul looks downward in dread and fear; remorse has possessed it. It looks on the right hand and the adamant walls keep it within its limits of torture. It looks on the left, and there the rampart of blazing fire forbids even a dreamy speculation of escape. It looks within and seeks consolation there, but a gnawing worm of guilt has entered into the soul. It looks around, but it has no friends to help, no comforters, but only tormenters, and they in abundance. It knows nothing of hope of deliverance. It has heard the everlasting key of God turning in its awful wards, and it has seen Him take that key and hurl it down into the depth of eternity, never to be found again. It does not hope, it knows no escape, it does not guess of deliverance. It pants for death, but death is too much its foe to be there. It longs that non-existence may swallow it up, but this eternal death is worse than annihilation. It pants for extermination as the laborer pants for his rest; it longs that it might be swallowed up in nothingness, but it does not come — there is only eternal death. When eternity shall have rolled around myriads of its everlasting cycles, it shall still be dead. Forever does not know any end; eternity cannot be spelled except in eternity. Still the soul cannot but see written over its head, 'You are condemned to be here forever.' It hears howlings that are to be perpetual; it sees flames which are unquenchable; it feels pains that are unmitigated; it hears a sentence that rolls on and on and on, shaking the echoes of eternity, making thousands of years shake again with the horrid thunder of its dreadful sound, *"Go away from Me, you cursed ones, into the everlasting fire which has been prepared for the devil and his angels"* — this is the eternal death.

## LIFE IN CHRIST

Secondly, there is life in Christ Jesus, for He says, *"You will not come to Me that you may have life."* There is no life in God the Father for a sinner; there is no life in God the Spirit for a sinner, apart from Jesus. The life of a sinner is in Christ. If you take the Father apart from the Son, though He loves His elect and has decreed that they shall live, yet He has ordained that life shall be only in His Son. If you take God the

Spirit apart from Jesus Christ, though it is the Spirit who gives us spiritual life, yet still it is life in Christ, life in the Son. We dare not and we cannot apply for spiritual life first to God the Father or to God the Holy Spirit. The first thing we are led to do when God brings us out of Egypt is this, we must eat the Passover Lamb — it is the very first thing. The first means by which we get life is by feeding on the flesh and blood of the Son of God; living in Him, trusting in Him, believing in His grace and power.

Our second thought was this, that there is life in Christ. We will show you that there are three kinds of life in Christ, just as there are three kinds of death.

## 1. LEGAL LIFE — NO CONDEMNATION

First, there is legal life in Christ. Just as every man by nature considered in Adam had a sentence of condemnation passed on him in the moment of Adam's sin, and more especially in the moment of his own first transgression, so I, if I am a believer, and you, if you also trust in Christ, have had a legal sentence of acquittal passed on us through what Jesus Christ has done. O condemned sinner, you may be sitting there condemned to death, like a prisoner in Newgate, but before this day has passed away you could be as clear from guilt as the pure angels above! There is such a thing as legal life in Christ; and, blessed be God, some of us enjoy it. We know our sins are pardoned because Christ suffered punishment for them. We know that we never can be punished ourselves, because Christ suffered in our place. The Passover is slain for us, the lintel and the door-post have been sprinkled, and the destroying angel can never touch us. For us there is no hell, although it may blaze with a terrible flame. Let Tophet be prepared of old, let its pile be wood and much smoke, we never can come there, for Christ has died for us, in our place. What if there are racks of horrid torture? What if there is a sentence producing horrible reverberations of thundering sounds in the souls of men? Yet there shall be no rack, no dungeon, no thunder for us. We are now delivered in Christ Jesus, *"There is therefore now no condemnation to us who are in Christ Jesus, who do not walk according to the flesh, but according to the Spirit."*

Sinner, you are legally condemned this morning. Do you feel that? Then let me tell you that faith in Christ will give you a knowledge of your legal acquittal. Beloved, it is no fancy that we are condemned for our sins, it is a reality. So it is not a fancy that we are acquitted, it is a reality. A man about to be hanged, if he received a full pardon would feel it to be a great reality. He would say, 'I have a full pardon, I cannot be touched now.' That is just how I feel.

Fellow-saints, we have gained legal life in Christ, and such legal life that we cannot lose it. The sentence has gone against us once, now it has gone out for us. It is written, *"There is now no condemnation,"* and that now will do as well for me in fifty years as it does now.

## 2. SPIRITUAL LIFE – A CORPSE MADE ALIVE

Then, secondly, there is spiritual life in Christ Jesus. As the man is spiritually dead, so God has spiritual life for him, for there is no need which is not supplied by Jesus, there is no emptiness in the heart which Christ cannot fill. There is no desolation which He cannot cause to teem with life; there is no desert which He cannot make to blossom as the rose. O dead sinners, you spiritually dead ones, there is life in Christ Jesus! Yes, these eyes have seen the dead come alive again; we have known men whose views were carnal, whose lusts were mighty, whose passions were strong, then suddenly, by the irresistible might of the Holy Spirit, they have thrown themselves completely on Jesus and have become a child of God. We know that there is life in Christ Jesus, life of a spiritual order. Yes, more, we ourselves in our own persons have felt that there is spiritual life. We can well remember when we sat in the house of prayer, as dead as the very seat on which we sat. We had listened for a long, long while to the sound of the gospel, but nothing had happened. Then suddenly, as if our ears had been opened by the fingers of some mighty angel, a sound entered our ears and went straight to our heart — we thought we heard Jesus crying out, *He that has ears to hear, let him hear!!"* Then an irresistible hand put itself on our heart and crushed a prayer out of it. We never had a prayer like that before! Then we cried out, *"O God, have mercy on me, a sinner!"*

Some of us for months felt a hand pressing us as if we had been crushed in a vice, and our souls bled drops of anguish. That misery was a sign of coming life. Persons being drowned do not feel the pain so much when they are being restored. O we remember those pains, those groans, that living strife which our soul had when it came to Christ. We can remember the giving of our spiritual life as easily as a man could remember being restored from the grave.

We can suppose that Lazarus remembered his resurrection, though perhaps not all the circumstances of it. So we, although we have forgotten a great deal, do remember the giving of ourselves to Christ. We can say to every sinner, however dead he may be, that there is life in Christ Jesus. He who has raised Lazarus has raised us. However rotten you may be in the grave of your sins, He can say even to you, *"Come out!"*

## 3. ETERNAL LIFE CAN NEVER BE LOST

In the third place, there is eternal life in Christ Jesus. And, oh, if eternal death is terrible, then how blessed must be eternal life! For He has said, *"Where I am, there My people shall be also;"* and, *"Father, I desire that those whom You have given Me may be with Me where I am, so that they may see My glory which You have given to Me."* This is He who also said, *"My sheep hear My voice and I know them. And they follow Me. And I give to them eternal life. And they shall never perish, nor shall anyone pluck them out of My hand."* (See John 17:23; 10:27,28)

Surely anyone with the Arminian doctrine of salvation must buy a pair of rubber lips if he is to preach from those texts, for I am sure he would need to stretch his mouth amazingly. He would never be able to speak the whole truth without winding about in a most mysterious manner. For eternal life is not a life which can be lost. If I lost life in Adam, I have gained it in Christ. If I lost myself forever, I find myself forever in Jesus Christ. Eternal life, O how blessed the thought! Our eyes will sparkle with joy and our souls burn with ecstasy in the thought that my soul will live in bliss and joy everlastingly. O sun, your eye can be put out, but my eye shall forever see the King in His beauty in a day when your eye shall no more be making the green earth laught. And O moon, be turned into blood! My blood shall never be turned to nothingness, this spirit of mine will exist when you have ceased to be. And O great world, you may all subside, just as a moment's foam subsides on the wave that bears it, but I shall have eternal life. O time, you may see giant mountains dead and hidden in their graves; you may see the stars like figs too ripe falling from the tree, but you shall never, never, never again see my spirit dead!

## GOD SAVES ALL WHO COME

This brings us to the third point, that eternal life is given to all who come for it. There never was a man who came to Christ for eternal life, for legal life, for spiritual life, who had not already received it, in some sense, and it was revealed to him that he had received it soon after he came. Let us take one or two texts: *"He is able to save to the uttermost those that come to Him."* Everyone who comes to Christ will find that Christ is able to save him — not able to save him a little, to deliver him from a little sin, to keep him from a little trial, to carry him a little way and then drop him — but able to save him to the uttermost extent of his sin, to the uttermost length of his trials, to the uttermost depths of his sorrows, to the uttermost duration of his existence. Christ says to everyone who comes to Him, 'Come, poor sinner, you need not ask whether I have power to save. I will not ask you how far you have gone into sin, for I am able to save you to the uttermost."

Now another text, *"All that the Father gives to Me SHALL come to Me, and HIM THAT COMES to Me I will in no way cast out"*(John

6:37). Take note that the promises are always to the coming ones. Anyone that comes shall find the door of Christ's house opened, yea, the door of his heart too. Everyone that comes, I say it in the broadest sense, shall find that Christ has mercy for him. The greatest absurdity in the world is to want to have a wider gospel than that which is recorded in the Scripture. I preach that everyone that believes SHALL be saved, that everyone who comes SHALL find mercy. People ask me such questions as this one, 'But suppose a man should come who was not chosen, would he be saved?' If you must suppose nonsense, expect no answer from me. If a man is not chosen, he will never come! When he does come, it is a sure sign that he was chosen! Another says, 'Suppose one should go to Christ who had not been called by the Spirit.' Stop right there! That is a supposition that you have no right to make, for such a thing cannot happen. You are only saying it to try to entangle me, and you will not do that just yet. I say that everyone who comes to Christ SHALL be saved. I can say that as a Calvinist, or if you insist, as a Hyper-Calvinist, as plainly as you can say it. My gospel is no more narrow than yours, whoever you are, but my gospel is laid on a solid foundation, whereas your gospel is built on nothing but sand and rottenness: *"No one CAN come to Me unless the Father who sent Me draw him, and I will raise him up at the last day"* (John 6:44) — therefore everyone who comes SHALL be saved.

But another says, 'suppose all the world would come, then would Christ receive them all?' Certainly, if all would come, He would — but, then, they won't all come. What I tell you is this, that all of those that DO COME shall be given eternal life. If they are as bad as devils, Christ will receive them if they come to Him. If they had all sin and filthiness running into their hearts like a common sewer for the whole world, Christ would receive them if they come. But they will not come to Him that they may have life, except the Father draw them.

## UNIVERSAL ATONEMENT A LIE

Another says, "I want to know about the rest of the people. May I go out and tell them that Jesus Christ died for every one of you? May I say that there is life for every one of you?' No, you may not! You may say there is life for every one that comes, but if you say that there is life for even one of those that will not come, then you utter a dangerous lie. If you tell them that Jesus Christ was punished for their sins, and yet they will be lost, you are telling them a willful lie! To think that God could first punish Christ, and then punish them — why, I wonder at your foolish daring to have the impudence to say so! A good man was once preaching that there were harps and crowns in Heaven for all in his congregation; and he wound up in a most solemn manner, saying, 'My dear friends, there are many for whom these things are prepared who will not get there.' In fact, he made such a pitiful tale of it as was possible. But I tell you that he should have been weeping for the angels of Heaven, and for all the saints, for if what he was saying was true, then Heaven would be spoiled through and through.

Think of the angels seeing crowns in Heaven gathering cobwebs, seeing empty thrones. They might begin talking to one another, saying, 'None of us are safe here, for the promise was that He would give all His sheep eternal life, yet there is a lot of those in hell that God gave eternal life to; there is a number burning in the pit for whom Christ shed His blood, and if they may be sent there, then so may we. For if we cannot trust one promise of God, we surely cannot trust another.' Why Heaven would lose its foundation and fall! Away with your nonsensical gospel! God gives us instead a safe and solid one, built on covenant doings and covenant relationships, on eternal purposes and sure fulfilments.

## NO ONE WILLS TO COME

This brings us to the fourth point, that by nature no one WILL come to Christ, for the text says plainly, *"You WILL NOT COME to Me, that you might have life."* I assert on Scripture authority from my text that you will not come to Christ in order that you might have life. I tell you that I could preach to you forever, I could borrow the eloquence of Demosthenes or of Cicero, but you will not come to Christ. I could beg you on my knees, with tears in my eyes; I could show you the horrors of hell and the joys of Heaven, the sufficiency of Christ and your own lost condition, but you would not one of you come to Christ of your own free will, you would not come unless the Spirit that rested on Christ should draw you. It is true of all men in their natural conditon that they WILL NOT come to Christ.

But I hear another of these babblers asking a question, saying, 'But could they not come if they wanted to come?' Yes, my friend, but the problem is that they are dead and do not want to come. But that is not the question this morning. I am talking about what they will do, not what they CAN do. You will notice when you talk about free will that the poor Arminian, in just two seconds, begins to talk about power. He mixes up two subjects that should be kept apart. We will not take two subjects at once. We decline to fight two battles at the same time. Another day we will preach that *"No one CAN come except the Father draw him."* But it is only the will that we have before us now. And it is certain that men WILL NOT COME to Christ that they might have life.

We could prove this from many texts of Scripture, but we will take one parable. You remember the parable where a certain king had a feast for his son and invited a great number to come. The oxen and fatlings were killed, and he sent his messengers to ask many to the supper. Did they go to the feast? No, but all of them, with one accord, began to make excuses. One said that he had married a wife, and therefore he could not come, whereas he could have brought her with him. Another had bought a yoke of oxen and wanted to try them out; but the feast was at night; could he have tried his oxen out only in the dark? Another had bought a piece of land and he wanted to go see it; but I do not think he could have seen much of it with a lantern. So they all made excuses and none of them would come. Well the king was determined to have the feast, so he said to them, *"Go out into the highways and hedges and compel them to come in"* – note that he did not say this time to invite them, but he said to 'compel' them. Even the ragged fellows in the hedges would never have come if they had not been compelled!

Take another parable: There was a certain man who had a vineyard. At the appointed time he sent one of his servants to collect the rent. What did they do to him? They beat that servant. Then he sent another, and they stoned him. He sent another and they killed him. And, at last, he said, *I will send my son, they will have respect for my son.* But what did they do? They said, *"This is the heir! Come, let us kill him and get hold of his inheritance. And taking him, they threw him out of the vineyard and killed him."* And it is the same with all men by nature. The Son of God came, yet men rejected Him.

### HOW FAR DID MEN FALL?

There is not time to mention the multitude of Scripture proofs, but we will refer to the great doctrine of the Fall. Anyone who believes that man's will is entirely free, that he can be saved by it, is one that does not really believe in the Fall. As I sometimes tell you, few preachers of religion truly believe the doctrine of the Fall, else they think that when Adam fell down he only broke his little finger and not his neck, that he fainted but did not fully ruin his race. Why, beloved, the Fall broke man up entirely. It did not leave one power unimpaired. All was shattered, debased and tarnished. Like some mighty temple, the pillars may be there, the shaft and the column, the pilaster might be there, but they are all broken and shattered, though some seem to retain their form and position. The conscience of man sometimes retains much of its tenderness, yet it is fallen. Neither is the will exempt. Though it may be 'the Lord Mayor of Mansoul,' as Bunyan calls it, yet the Lord Mayer goes wrong. The Lord Will-be-will was continually doing wrong.

Your fallen nature was put out of order; your will, among other things, has completely gone astray from God. But I tell you what will be the best proof of that, it is that great fact that you never did meet a Christian in your life who ever said he came to Christ without Christ coming to him.

## THERE ARE NO 'FREE-WILL' PRAYERS

I dare say you have heard a great many Arminian sermons, but you have never heard an Arminian prayer. For the saints in prayer appear as one, in word and in deed and in mind. An Arminian on his knees would pray desperately like a Calvinist. He cannot pray about free-will, for there is no room for it. Can you imagine him praying, 'Lord, I thank You that I am not like those poor presumptuous Calvinists. Lord, I was born with a glorious free-will; I was born with power by which I can turn to You of myself; I have improved my grace. If everybody had done the same with their grace that I have done with mine, then they all might have been saved. Lord, I know You do not make us willing if we are not first willing ourselves. You give grace to everybody; some do not improve it, but I do. There are many that will go to hell as much bought with the blood of Christ as I was; they had as much of the Holy Spirit given to them as I; they had as good an opportunity and were as much blessed as I am. It was not Your grace that made us to differ; I know it did a great deal, still I turned the point; I made use of what was given me, and others did not — that is the difference between me and them.'

That is a prayer for the devil, for nobody else would offer such a prayer as that. Ah, when they are preaching and talking slowly, there may be wrong doctrine. But when they come to pray, the true thing slips out, they cannot help it. If a man talks very slowly, he may speak in a fine manner; but when he comes to talk fast, the old brogue of his country, where he was born, slips out.

I ask you again, did you ever meet a Christian man who said, "I came to Christ without the power of the Spirit"? If you ever did meet such a man, you need have no hesitation in saying, 'I believe it, and I believe you went away without the power of the Spirit, and I believe that you know nothing about the matter, that you are still in the gall of bitterness and in the bond of iniquity.' Do I hear one Christian saying, 'I sought Jesus before He sought me; I went to the Spirit, and the Spirit did not come to me first'? No, beloved, we are obliged, each one of us, to put our hands to our hearts and say, 'Grace taught my soul to pray and my eyes overflow; it was grace that kept me to this day and will not let me go.' Is there one who can say, 'I sought God before He sought me'? No, even you who are a little Arminian will sing, 'O yes! I do love Jesus, because He first loved me.'

Then, one more question. Do we not find, even after we have come to
Christ, our soul is not free, but is kept by Christ? Do we not find times,
even now, when to will is not present with us? There is a law in our
members which wars against the law of our minds. Now, if those who
are spiritually alive feel that their will is contrary to God, what shall we
say of the man who is dead in trespasses and sins? It would be a
marvelous absurdity to put the two on a level. And it would be still
more absurd to put the dead before the living. No, the text is true,
experience has branded it into our hearts, *"You will not come to Me
that you might have life."*

## WHY DO NONE COME?

Now we must tell you the reasons why men will not come to Christ.
The first is this, that no man by nature thinks that he needs Christ. He
thinks that he has a robe of righteousness of his own, that he is
welldressed, that he is not naked, that he has no need of Christ's blood
to wash him, that he is not black or crimson, and no grace is needed to
purify him. No one knows his need until God shows him his need. No
one will seek a pardon until the Holy Spirit reveals the necessity for a
pardon. I may preach Christ forever, but unless you feel you need
Christ you will never come to Him. A doctor may have a good shop,
but no one will buy his medicines until he feels he needs them.

The next reason is this, that men do not like Christ's way of saving
them. One says, 'I do not like it because he makes me holy; I cannot
drink or swear any longer if He saved me.' Another says, 'It requires me
to be so precise and puritanical, and I like a little more license.'
Another does not like it because it is so humbling; he does not like it
because the gate of Heaven is not quite high enough for his head, and
he does not like to stoop. That is the chief reason you will not come to
Christ, because you cannot get to him with your heads straight up in
the air. For Christ makes you stoop when you come to Him. Another
does not like it to be grace from first to last that saves. He says, 'Oh if I
might have a little honor.' But when he hears it is all Christ or no
Christ, a whole Christ or no Christ, he says, 'I shall not come,' and he
turns on his heel and goes away. Ah, proud sinners, you WILL NOT
come to Christ! Ah, ignorant sinners, you WILL NOT come to Christ
because you know nothing of Him. And that is the third reason. Men
do not know His worth, for if they did they would come to Him. Why
did not sailors go to America before Columbus went? Because they did
not believe there was an America. Columbus had faith, so he went. He
who has faith in Christ goes to Him. But you do not know Jesus; many
of you have never seen His beautiful face; you have never seen how

applicable His blood is to a sinner, how great His atonement is and how all-sufficient His merits are. Therefore you will not come to Him.

## THERE IS NO EXCUSE FOR ANYONE NOT TO COME TO CHRIST

My last thought is a solemn one. I have preached that you will not come. But some will say, 'It is their sin that they do not come.' It is so. You will not come, but then your will is a sinful will. Some think that we 'sew pillows to all armholes' when we preach this doctrine, but we do not. We do not set this down as being part of man's original nature, but as belonging only to his FALLEN nature. It is sin that has brought you into this condition that you will not come to Christ. If you have never fallen, you would come to Christ the moment He is preached to you. But you do not come because of your sinfulness and crime. People excuse themselves because they have bad hearts. That is the most flimsy excuse in the world. Do not robbery and thieving come from bad hearts. Then suppose a thief would say to a judge, 'I could not help it, I had a bad heart'? What would the judge say? 'You rascal! Why, if your heart is bad, I'll make the sentence heavier, for you are a villain indeed. Your excuse is nothing.' The Almighty shall *"laugh at them and shall have them in derision."* We do not preach this doctrine to excuse you, but to humble you. The possession of a bad nature is my fault as well as my terrible calamity.

It is a sin that will always be charged to men: when they will not come to Christ, it is sin that keeps them away. He who does not preach this truth is not, I fear, faithful to God and his own conscience. Go home, then, with this thought, 'I am by nature so perverse that I will not come to Christ, and that wicked perversity of my nature is my sin. I deserve to be sent to hell for it.' And if the thought does not humble you, the Spirit using it, no other can.

May God humble us all. Amen.

Charles Haddon Spurgeon

# 'FREE-WILL'

by

Jay Green

Men love to claim the right of 'free-will.' In the beginning, we read that God permitted Adam that freedom of will which so many have since coveted. That is, He allowed Adam to choose to do whatever he wanted most to do. And what did Adam use his freedom of will to choose? He immediately chose sin, the pleasing of himself instead of God. Adam was free, he was pure; he was intelligent, wise and righteous. Yet he chose evil freely! He had never sinned, he was sinless at the time the choice was presented to him, yet he willed to sin. Why? Whatever you do, do not be so wicked as to blame God. For here you see that even a good man's will is apt to choose against his own Maker when he is cut loose from God's powerful influence for good. And if even a good man is capable of choosing to be a god to himself, will you who are *"only evil continually"* (Gen. 6:5) then proudly claim that you are free and independent of God's predetermining will? Are you then, like Adam, claiming to be free to choose to be your own god, with the right even to nullify God's rights and God's power?

That you may see in black and white that sinful men do claim such things, here is one man's statement, "Unfortunately, God has no power over the will of man. That is to say, He cannot save a person against his will, but at the same time, He is not willing that any should perish. He has made it possible for all men to be saved. But the Bible indicates that salvation depends upon man's willingness to be saved. It would be a kind of tyranny if God saved people against their will...." —Billy Graham, as quoted by *The Standard Bearer*, Grand Rapids, 11/66.

It is not scriptural to talk about God saving anyone against his will, and it is surely bordering on blasphemy to mention tyranny and God in the same sentence. God makes His people willing in the day of His power (Ps. 110:3). Yes, He even puts in them the will to do all that He pleases. This claim of man that his will must not be violated or frustrated, except by his consent, runs head-on into innumerable statements to the contrary in Scripture. Where in the Bible have you ever

[This is an excerpt from Mr. Green's book, *God's Everlasting Love*, which has sold tens of thousands of copies, changing many lives.]

read that it is man's will that is done in Heaven or on earth. On the contrary, it is written, *"And all the people of the earth are counted as nothing. And He does according to His will in the army of Heaven, and among the people of the earth. And no one can strike His hand, or say to Him, What are you doing?"* (Daniel 4:35). The limitations which the evil imaginations of men put on God's will cannot be found on any page of His Holy Word, therefore it is certain that a mere claim of independence by a sinful creature (with a very obvious ax to grind) cannot limit God a whit, nor keep Him from doing what He pleases with you, or to you, or within you. He can change your mind, or He can change your heart!

It is true that God loved Adam, for He loved all His creation. But in Adam's case, He set His love on him for a foredetermined period. As with us, this love of Adam did not leave God strapped, let alone trapped— He did not give up His freedom of will and make it subject thereafter to the will of man. He was not a man that He should be so in love and so involved that He could not extricate Himself from entanglement in a love affair that went wrong. He is GOD! He is the God who predestinated the Fall and every other happening in this world from the beginning to the end, *"according to the purpose of Him who works all things according to the counsel of His OWN will"* (Ephesians 1:11). The foundation of the Lord has not been breached, it still stands firm, having this seal, *"The Lord knows those that are His"* (2 Timothy 2:19).

Billy Graham tells us that "the Bible indicates that salvation depends upon man's willingness to be saved;" but *"salvation is of God,"* therefore GOD tells us that *"After He had willed it, He brought us forth by the word of truth,"* (James 1:18) for *"faith is a gift of God, and that not of yourselves, lest any man should boast,"* (Ephesians 3:8) *"so then it is not of him that wills or of him that runs, but of God who shows mercy"* (Romans 9:16) for those that believe were *"not born of blood, nor of the will of man, but were born of God"* (John 1:12). We do not love Him because we first willed to do so, but *"we love Him because He first loved us"* (1 John 4:19). Not all are His; not all are sons; not all are loved with an everlasting love:

1. NOT ALL ARE HIS, for when God says that He *"knows those that are His,"* He then teaches that there are some that are not His. To know a person, in Scripture, is to love that person, as a search of your concordance will prove. And it is obvious that in 2 Timothy 2:19 God is telling that there are certain persons He knows in the way of love. He has knowledge of all persons, not merely those that are His. Furthermore, if there are those He knows, then there are also those He does not know. If there is a group which HE designates as *"those that are His,"* then there must be a group which certainly cannot be included in those that are His.

2. NOT ALL ARE SONS, for then it would not be necessary for men to obtain the adoption which enables them to cry, *"Abba, Father."*

3. NOT ALL ARE LOVED, for God hates the wicked every day. He hated Esau, He hates the workers of iniquity, etc. The Scriptures abound with those said to be hated by our God (See Psalm 5:5; 11:5; Romans 9)

For example, the Lord says that He chastens every one He loves. But are all chastened? God says no, for He says that *"He scourges every son whom He receives"* (Hebrews 12:6,7). Not all are sons, not all are received, not all are chastened; and these are the marks of God's love. He is the One who makes the difference between us, not we ourselves: *"But if you are without chastisement, of which all* (sons) *are partakers, then you are bastards and not sons"* (Hebrews 12:8). So there are those who are not loved and not chastised, and they are here called illegitimate. *"Bastards"* have another father than do *"Beloved sons"*: *"You are of father — the devil!"* (John 8:44). Some are God's sons; some are sons of the devil. The proof in one case is this, that if God chastises, they are His.

It is true, of course, that we are all the offspring of God, His creatures. But that does not make all creatures to be sons of love that are chastised. All men enter this world under condemnation, and thus are born to trouble. Not all trouble, however, is chastisement — some is affliction for punishment. God makes a difference between men and men. Some He adopts as sons; these He chastises to make them better children. Others He afflicts with a never-ending punishment for their sins. To these He shows no love: they are not chastised, they are never given the gift of faith which would be unto justification and adoption into God's family. Why are these things so? Is it not because it seemed good in God's sight? Is it not because it was according to His original purpose?

## THREE QUESTIONS IN REGARD TO 'FREE-WILL'

1. Is it possible for a creature to have a free will and to continually exercise that will in complete conformity to the will of God?

2. Are the creatures who thus conform their wills continually to the will of God in servitude? Are they mere slaves?

3. If God plans, foredetermines and predestinates each and every deed of a man's life, powerfully controlling all circumstances, all persons, even all forces of whatever variety and magnitude that affects his life, can that man be truly free?

1. Yes, it is possible to do God's will continually, without interruption, without even the opportunity to do one's own separate planning, yet at the same time to be absolutely and perfectly free.

The angels in God's presence are creatures. They were created with the ability to will, they were and are free agents in the use of that will, yet they continually use their wills to do what God desires for them to do, and only what He wills for them to do (Psalm 103:20,21). Do you think the good angels serve God with rebellion in their hearts? No, they freely will to please God, and that without ceasing. The angels can be shown to have freedom of will by the fact that some of them in a fit of pride chose to please themselves instead of God. God permitted them this foolish exercise of their wills for His own wise purposes, even though their free choice made them certain occupants of Hell forever. Yes, the *"elect angels"* (1 Timothy 5:21) continue to have free-will.

2. Yes again, even though your will is perfectly and continually conformed to God's will, you have freedom. To always and forever do the

will of God, without any interruption to please yourself, is the ultimate freedom which may be conferred on any creature! This was God's purpose in creating you. All things and persons are created for His glory, and for the purpose of fulfilling His will, and only HIS will. Man, when created, was so disposed. Animals are programmed to do exactly what God predestinated them to do. For His own purposes God was pleased to create men and angels with a will. In creating them, however, He definitely disposed their wills to joyfully fulfill His will. In addition to this freedom of will and disposition to use it aright, God gave power to exercise this will by a continual forthputting of His own power within them and upon them. He powerfully imposed His great "I will" on their wills in order to keep them pure, perfect and happy (for happiness is nothing more than the fulfilling of the purpose for which you were made, and both men and angels were made simply and only for God's glory and purpose).

In the case of the elect angels, God never intermitted His power; He kept them ever happily willing to do only what pleased Him. In the case of the fallen angels, He simply left them with their created wills, their created power. They used this creature power to will to do evil; that is, they decided to do things differently than what God willed. Fallen men also became the condemned creatures they are by being left to their own power and will. Adam, and all men in Adam, sinned and came short of the glory of God. Is this the essence of freedom? Must one be free to do evil in order for him to be truly free?

The elect angels are still free, even though God has not permitted them to fall into sin. They have maintained their freedom and joy in doing the will of God, through all the ages. *"O Lord, You are worthy to receive glory and honor and power"* is the way they think and act. Is this servitude? No, for servitude is a state of involuntary subjection to a master. These serve the Master voluntarily.

Are the elect angels slaves? No, for a slave has no will of his own (per Webster). Fallen men and fallen angels are slaves to their lusts, and in the case of men, they are doubly slaves. For men are both slaves to Satan and slaves to their lusts. It is this very dedication to the cause of Satan that causes fallen men to be also doubly enemies of God. This is why they claim that a creature MUST have the right to be free from God's minute control over their lives. It is not just freedom of the will, but to godhood that they aspire. This claim that God has no right to put forth His power in order to cause them to do only and exactly His will is no more nor less than open rebellion against the rightful Maker and Master of men. Even in rebellion, they have no freedom nor right to attempt to thwart the will of God. And any attempt to elevate the will of man to the height and level of the will of God is in effect an attempt to thwart the will of God. Any success that men may claim in this warfare with God is strictly in their own evil imaginations. God still rules the wills of all men, their actions, their lives, and their fellow-conspirators — all to cause His will to be done without interference, interruption, or ceasing.

# AN IRREFUTABLE EXAMPLE OF GOD'S WILL REIGNING

*"For God has put into their hearts to fulfill His will, and to agree, and to give their kingdoms to the beast, until the words of God shall be fulfilled"* (Revelation 17:17). Here are multitudes of people. They all have wills. They are all free agents. Also to a man they are traitors to God, they are His enemies. As such they despise the will of God; in fact, they are determined not to do His will at all costs. Yet these evil people, so bent on fulfilling their own rebellious wills, are said to agree to do the will of God! Yea, more, it is said that *God has put into their hearts* this agreement to fulfill His will. Still more, they did at the same time fulfill their own evil wills and the good will of God, by giving their kingdoms to the beast — and all this so that and until *the words of God were fulfilled.* Were they then not free to act? Did this sudden willingness, so contrary to their normal bent and behavior, make them slaves to God? When their evil will had come up against the will of God, was God in any way frustrated by the fact that they determined to do their own wills? Did God change His will in order to accommodate the will of any of these evil men? Did not God rather change THEIR will in order to cause them to agree to His? If language has any meaning, and if the Bible is at all credible, then we must assign some meaning to these words of God, *"GOD has put into their hearts to fulfill HIS will..."*

Now you can see the stark nakedness of the lie which says that the vaunted and much-publicized 'free' will of man is permitted to defy God and stand out against His revealed will. It can be seen here that the conclusion that man's will is proven to be independently free, because he is permitted to do what his evil heart desires, is a delusion. Certainly, the foolish notion that "God has no power over the will of man," as quoted, is directly contradicted by the plain and unmistakeable words of God in this verse, *"For GOD has put into their hearts to fulfill HIS will,"* etc.

Rivers of unbelief and rebellion may indeed flow freely from the bowels of men, but they are not in any way free to thwart the will of God: (1) Men do indeed devise and plot the steps they choose to follow, but it is the Lord who directs his actual steps. A man may lie awake all night engraving mischievous plans on his memory, but the plan he selects and follows is within the plan of God from everlasting. It is God that disposes the man to perform strictly according to His purpose (Read Proverbs 15:11; 16:4; 16:9; 16:33). Even if the man is hung up with doubt and throws dice as an easy way to decide which mischief to do, God disposes him to exactly be in line with His eternal plan (Proverbs 16:33). *"It is not in man to direct his own steps"* (Jeremiah 10:23) — it is God that puts into their hearts to do what He wills.

The thought which wells up into the mind of men at this point is this: Does this not then make God the author of sin? Such an unclean thought should be unthinkable — no pure creature would ever dare to think it — only men and devils, of all creatures, have been wicked enough to ever ask that self-condemning question. Paul answers it in Romans 9:19, *"Yes, rather, O man, who are you that answers against God? Shall the thing formed say to Him who formed it, Why did you make me this way? Or, does not the potter have authority over the clay, out of the same lump to make one vessel to honor and another to dishonor? And* what *if God, intending to show wrath and to make His power known, endured with much longsuffering the vessels of wrath fitted for destruction? And* also *that He might make known the riches of His glory on vessels of mercy which He BEFOREHAND PREPARED FOR GLORY"* (Romans 9:20-23).

It must be remembered that *"God made man upright"* (Ecclesiastes 7:29). God did not make, He could not make any creature evil. Man made himself a sinner. James clearly depicts what happened to Adam and to all men in Adam, *"Let no one say when he is tempted, It is because I am tempted of God. For God cannot be tempted by evils, and He Himself tempts no one. But each one is tempted when he is drawn away and seduced by his own lust. Then when lust has conceived, it gives birth to sin. And when it is fully finished, sin brings forth death"* (James 1:13-15). Man seduces himself with evil desires. Satan helps. Consider the case of David numbering the people against God's command: In one view from the Scriptures, it is attributed to David's sin (2 Samuel 24:10); in another view, to Satan's provocation (1 Chronicles 21:1); yet in still another place it is said to be according to God's plan to test David (2 Samuel 24:1). The evil will of David was done, the sly will of Satan was done, and the perfect will of God (His secret will) was done! Yet God did not either tempt or force David to sin. Satan was not permitted to force David to follow his pride. Yet David did both the will of God and the will of Satan. How? Satan knew what was in man, and he set his bait accordingly. David followed his natural pride, acting according to the plan of Satan.

Do not men blame their misdeeds on Satan? Is there not a proverb among us which says, 'The devil made me do it'? Is this not an admission that Satan does indeed take men captive at HIS will? Where then is that 'free' will which they claim for themselves? Why then do they detest the thought that God is able to use His creative knowledge of man to close all the doors of the mind except that one which follows His foreordained plan? In both cases, it is man's evil nature which causes him to choose to do evil (See Genesis 6:5-8; Isaiah 64:6; Job 15:14-16; Eccles. 9:3).

## AN EXAMPLE OF FREE CHOICE, YET MASTERLY CONTROL

Consider this one natural example, then the results of this discussion will be left to God: Among rats there is none good, no, not one. Rats would not agree to this, but it is a fact known to superior men. Men cultivate and use rats for the benefit of mankind. In the laboratory men plan careful experiments, using rats according to their purposes, sometimes for their own glory. Mazes are constructed by scientists, who use the utmost of their intelligence, who carefully employ the total knowledge they have of rats and their behavior patterns. Since rats have an insatiable lust for food, this is used to cause the rats to perform the exact acts which the scientist desires. If the scientist is wise, if he knows his rats, they will perform feats that amaze other men, thus giving glory to that scientist. The rat knows and cares nothing about all this; he is simply and only interested in fulfilling his lust, and he will use the utmost of his intelligence and cunning to get what he wants. The scientist actually has complete control over the rat's acts; he knows exactly where he will be, when he will be there, what he will do there. He knows rats, and he constructs his maze with a skill that comes from superior knowledge. Yet the rat is not in any way influenced in his actions by the unseen superior who has planned his entire life, every action from birth to death. The rat still does what all the other rats agree is intelligent and right: he acts like a rat. *He naturally will choose those courses of action which are pleasing to his rat-nature.* It perhaps would be true that he would protest vigorously if he knew he was under control, that he was exactly fulfilling his superior's will, especially that part of his will which thwarted the immediate lust of the rat. But in no case would the scientist be concerned over the rat's protest. He is so far superior to the rat, which he bred and reared for a good purpose, that he will not in any way alter his thinking, his plans or his acts to mollify the rat. The rat has no better purpose than to fulfill the plan and purpose of his superior master, man.

Men are not rats, being far superior in reason and innumerable additional attributes. They are also superior in God's purpose. But rats have become superior to men; or, rather, man has sinned and made himself inferior to the rat, the horse, and other animals in this respect, that the animals willingly do what God has planned for them to do. But men by the evil nature which they have brought on themselves by sin do God's will unwillingly.

But the main point to be noted here is this: that a man is not nearly so superior to a rat as God is superior to a man!

If man has the right to breed and use rats for the good of mankind, and if this is because men are given dominion over rats and are so far superior to rats by creation, then why do men blaspheme God? Men, like rats, by nature follow the dictates of their own heart's lusts. Like rats, a spirit of frustration and anger arises when they are thwarted. But God is just in His treatment of men, allowing them to make their own choices, arranging circumstances so that those choices fulfill the will of their Maker, all the while plainly revealing to man his evil nature. Yet man proudly reacts to the goodness and mercy of God by trying to dethrone his Benefactor. He is even willing to lie and to affirm that *"there is no God"* (Psalm 14:1). Or he will pretend that God has painted Himself into a corner so foolishly as to now have to obey the decision of man — all this in order to fulfill his own evil lusts. But God continues to be pure, faithful, good and merciful to His creature, though he is no longer willing to be in God's image — he must needs now be his own god.

How wonderful it is that God has chosen some among men to love with an everlasting love, *"Yes, I have loved you with an everlasting love"*

(Jeremiah 31:3)! He did not choose angels, or rats, but men. Rejoice not that you have superiorities over rats, or other evil-natured men, but that God has chosen men for His purpose of showing how wise, powerful, pure, faithful, loving and glorious He truly is.

(2) Before a man consciously performs an act to fulfill his own plan and purpose, that plan is subjected, usually unconsciously, to Satan's scrutiny, as well as to God's. Natural men have Satan as their king (Eph. 2:1-3) and are captive to his will (2 Tim. 2:26). A true child of God escapes this, being hedged in by the word of God and his faithfulness to it, which makes Satan flee. But he is not born free from a devil's direction. As long as he is bent on doing his own will, instead of rightfully seeking out and obeying God's will, Satan is able to control him by appealing to those evil lusts which he has retained from his evil nature.

(3) There is an order established by God: God's will comes first, then He tells Satan exactly what he can and cannot do (Job 1:12; 2:6). Satan, in turn, must control the men and demons he employs, for they cannot be allowed to go beyond God's commands.

However, when a man becomes a new creature, beginning with a new heart, becoming a partaker of the divine nature, then all things become new. This means that his will also becomes new (2 Corinthians 5:17). For the first time this man, now a new man, finds the will to please God and the desire to submit his will to God's will. It is still necessary for him to say, with the apostle Paul, *"I know that in me (that is, in my flesh) dwells no good"* — but when the new man is made alive, he says, *"I delight in the law of God according to the inward man"* (Rom. 7:18,22). Still he is far from being able to say, "my will be done," so he must say, *"For to will is present with me, but how to work out the good I do not find"* and, *"O wretched man that I am! Who shall deliver me from the body of this death?"* (vss. 18, 24). Then how is his will to do good finally done? He answers, *"I thank God through Jesus Christ our Lord."* It is by the power of God working in him that the child of God is able to perform his will to do good, as God tells us, *"It is God that works in you to WILL and to do of HIS good pleasure"* (Philippians 2:13).

How does God create the will to do good? First, He takes away the stony heart which refuses to obey God (Ezekiel 36:26). Secondly, He gives a new capacity to perform His will, a new nature (2 Corinthians 5:17). Lastly, He then works mightily from time to time to create desires within us to do His will: *"who believe according to the working of His mighty strength"* (Ephesians 1:19). He also powerfully provides all the skill and means necessary for us to obey His commands, *"I will put My Spirit within you and CAUSE YOU to walk in My statutes"* (See Ezekiel 36:25-27 and Jeremiah 31:33,34).

In summation of this point, let it be clear that, (1) the elect angels have a will, but they are kept by the power of God so that they never will to do evil; their will is a free will, even though they are never permitted by God to will either an evil thought or a wicked act. (2) The fallen angels have a will, but having willed to please themselves instead of God, they became totally depraved and hopelessly evil. They have free agency: that is, they are free to choose, but only between evils; they are not free to choose anything good because their God-despising natures have neither desire, capacity or power to will to do good. They, like men, are slaves to sin. But unlike men, they have no salvation and no hope in a Savior. The difference in the freedom of will of elect angels and fallen angels is important. Some have missed the point that elect angels are kept free by the power of God, but that it is NOT the power of God which keeps fallen angels from being free — it is the power of sin, supplied by their own evil spirits, that keep fallen angels from the joys of being free to choose good. (3) Fallen men, likewise have a will. But imitating Satan, whose lusts they desired to do (John 8:44), they willfully displeased God by seeking to be gods. They also lost all goodness and freedom to choose God's will rather than their own. Now *"there is not one good, no, not one that seeks after God"* (Romans 3:10-12) unless and until God recreates in them a new heart, a new nature, and thus a new will. These do not desire to be good, do not obey the commands of God, but instead reject the things of the Spirit of God (1 Corinthians 2:14). *"Their hearts are fully set in them to do evil continually"* (Ecclesiastes 9:3), they are at enmity with God and cannot find it within themselves to be subject to His laws (which reflect His revealed will). (4) But new men in Christ Jesus have a will, a desire, a capacity to will that which is good and pleasing to God. And in their case, also, God supplies the power for them to do so. Being still weighted down with sin, a forthputting of God's power is required before they exercise their will to please God.

### CAN MAN'S ACTS BE FREE IF GOD PREDETERMINES THEM?

3. The best illustration of them all is usually the great Example of all: Jesus had a free will. Never was any man's will so free as the will of Jesus. He was truly man, a Man among men, the holiest, the wisest, the most powerful one that ever walked on this earth. Furthermore, He absolutely maintained complete independence among men; no one, either demon or man, could influence His actions so as to cause Him to veer from the course He had before-determined to be best. There was nothing in Him by which He could be moved to do anything but His own will. In every creational way He was a man. He was in every way subject to the same laws and restrictions that all men by creation were under. Here, then, was a man whose rights could not be violated, because He had violated no rights. Jesus had surrendered none of His rights by sin. He had a right to choose what He would, and He had a right to receive what He chose. Is there anyone, even among proud men, so far depraved that he will stand up and claim that he has as much right to have his own will done as Jesus did? No! For no sinner could ever have any such right.

What, then, can we say about the freedom of this excellent and truly deserving man, Christ Jesus? He, for one, could do as He pleased. Yet His entire life was minutely planned by God! Without the slightest deviation, He must inevitably, eternally devote every second of His life to the exact fulfilling of God's preordained plan. Do you deny either? Do deny that He could do as He pleased? Do you deny that He was under absolute necessity to exactly fulfill God's plan both in thought and in deed? If you deny either, you will wrest all hope of salvation from all men forever. If He did not fulfill God's prophecies and plans, then He sinned and has no righteousness to give to men. If His actions were not voluntary, they cannot be credited to us. His whole life was predetermined, yet He was absolutely free!

Then must we not conclude this, that a man may be an absolutely free man even while he is doing all that God has planned for him? God may preordain and foredetermine every thought and act of a man without in any way making him a slave without a will. And that man may exercise freedom of choice in every act of his life, even while he perfectly and completely fulfills God's predestined plan. See it proven in Jesus' life:

*"Men of Israel, hear these words. Jesus of Nazareth, a MAN approved of God among you by mighty works and wonders and miracles, which God worked by Him among you, as you yourselves know — this One was delivered to you BY THE BEFORE-DETERMINED COUNSEL AND FOREKNOWLEDGE OF GOD, and you laid your wicked hands on Him and killed Him, crucifying Him"*—Acts 2:22,23

*"For indeed both Herod and Pontius Pilate, with the heathen and the peoples of Israel, were gathered together against your holy child Jesus, whom You anointed, to do WHATEVER YOUR HAND AND COUNSEL BEFORE-DETERMINED TO BE DONE"*—Acts 4:27, 28.

In the first place you see Jesus being delivered by God's wisdom into wicked hands in order that God's plan for His crucifixion and death might be fulfilled. Then in the second place you see all the ungodly gathering together of their own will in order to do this dastardly deed. They were not herded together and driven to do this merciless murder by God's power, yet they were in every particular doing that which God had wisely determined should be done. Were they slaves to God in doing so? Or were they not rather slaves to Satan? Did he not take them captive at his will? Yes, but only because they were slaves to their own lusts! They were slaves both to Satan and to their own lusts. But even so, their acts were voluntary, freely chosen by themselves (in the sense of free-agency) yet for all of that, an exact fulfillment of God's plan took place in their lives. Just as surely as the predestined time had come for Jesus to give His life, so the predestinated time had come for them to take His life. For here in the third place you see Jesus acting freely, voluntarily choosing that ignominious, shameful death. He had said that He had power to lay down His life, and that He had power to take it up again. He was free to do so. Yet he was under necessity to fulfill the plan of God. He was predestinated, then prophesied to be the Lamb slain, before the foundation of the world. Not a single thought of His could wander away from God's will and plan.

How then do men say that they are not free if God predestinates and chooses beforehand what He will accomplish by them? Was Jesus not free? Shall sinners demand more freedom than the sinless Son of God?

To sum up this point, (1) God's predestination does not affect a man's freedom of choice, for he is left free to act according to his nature. A vulture standing before a rotting body and a bushel of good clean corn may be said to have a free choice as to what he will eat. But everyone knows beforehand what he will choose to eat, for it is the nature of vultures to love rottenness and to despise cleanness. He could live on either, but he prefers rottenness because of his nature. The fact that God planned for him to be a scavenger did not in any way affect his choice. Now even the vulture has his nature because of sin, for if there had been no sin there would have been no corruption (*"death is the wages of sin"*), and without corruption there would be no corrupt food for the vulture to eat. How much more, then, is man the victim of his own sin, having corrupted his nature to the point where God has said that *"he drinks iniquity like water,"* and that *"every imagination of his heart is only evil continually"* (Job 15:16; Genesis 6:5). It is not God's predestination, nor His creation, which limits the choice of men to that which is evil, but it is rather his own choice, his determination to be independent of God, which made him of an evil nature.

This, then, is the situation now: men still have the freedom to choose, but they no longer have a nature which desires good (good = that which pleases God); therefore man has free-agency, but he does not have freedom from God's control nor freedom to choose good. Jesus also had this free-agency, having a freedom which has been enjoyed only by the two sinless men ever on earth (Jesus and Adam). But Jesus did not have even a split second when His thoughts or His actions were not minutely planned so as to exactly fulfill the will and plan of God. He was sinless, perfect in every respect, as independent as any man could ever be, yet He never once desired, much less considered, independence from God's control. Why? Because He was not a sinner!

The wicked acts of men are charged against them even while they are in the act of exactly fulfilling the secret will of God. Do you think that those who hated, misjudged, and then murdered the blessed Lord Jesus Christ were not held strictly accountable for their evil thoughts and acts, their wicked conspiracy against God? God clearly condemns them.

## TO INSIST UPON FREE-WILL IS TO CRUCIFY CHRIST AFRESH

*It was not by the will of the flesh, not by the will of man that any person has been born of God and made a new creature in Christ Jesus. You not only deny such scriptures as John 1:13; Rom. 9:16, 21-23, when you insist you must first will before Christ can enter your heart, but you crucify Him afresh, putting Him to an open shame (Heb. 6:6), saying in effect that except your will be completely free from His control, and that you then freely exercise it before God the Holy Spirit gives you life and faith, then He has died in vain! In short, you are saying it is YOUR will which determines the extent, the effect, and the value of Christ's sacrifice. You are the imperious determiner of destiny: God can not predestinate, except by your will! Can there be a more stinking and nauseous example of the sinful PRIDE of man? Let God be true!*

Printed in the United States
150661LV00014B/48/A

9 781878 442574